Fail-Safe
Management

Fail-Safe Management

Five Rules to Avoid Project Failure

Jody Zall Kusek, Marelize Görgens Prestidge,
and Billy C. Hamilton

THE WORLD BANK
Washington, D.C.

Library of Congress Cataloging-in-Publication Data
Kusek, Jody Zall
  Fail safe management : five rules to avoid project failure / Jody Zall Kusek, Marelize Görgens Prestidge, and Billy C. Hamilton.
    pages cm
  Includes bibliographical references.
  ISBN 978-0-8213-9896-8 (alk. paper) — ISBN 978-0-8213-9897-5
  1. Project management.   2. Business failures.   I. Hamilton, Billy C.   II. World Bank.
III. Title.
  HD69.P75K87 2013
  658.4'04--dc23

                                                          2013009646

CONTENTS

FOREWORD

Managers who tackle tough problems have to be optimists. The hard shocks of reality so often can undermine their best efforts, and big investments of time and energy can lead to crushing failure. In fact, analysis of implementation—a careful look at how things get done (or don't) can sometimes seem like a trip to the pathologist's table, searching for clues about why a patient died. That sometimes makes it extra hard to be optimistic. In fact, one of the classic studies of implementation, by Jeffrey L. Pressman and Aaron Wildavsky in 1973, about a California economic development program, had one of the most depressing subtitles of all time: *How Great Expectations in Washington Are Dashed in Oakland; or, Why It's Amazing That Federal Programs Work at All*. And the subtitle goes on: *This Being a Saga of the Eeonomic Development Administration as Told by Two Sympathetic Observers Who Seek to Build Morals on a Foundation of Ruined Hopes*. How can managers be optimistic if they believe that it's amazing that anything works—and that the best they can hope for is gleaning morals from catastrophe?

That sad and cynical analysis dovetails with the tales of failure that tumble from blogs and newspaper pages. So often, it *does* seem amazing that programs work at all. But if that's the case, how can managers be optimistic? How can they build careers dedicated to producing results if the odds are stacked against them?

The great contribution of this wonderful and useful book lies in its invaluable tools to escape that trap. As the authors conclude, "Problems are inevitable in any development program; failure is not." And how to avoid failure? They provide five simple rules, supported by common-sense explanations and rich examples. When red tape threatens to bog down a process, good managers can push away the bottlenecks. When hierarchy clogs work, informal networks provide invaluable support. Good managers know not only their friends but also their critics, and they keep them both close. It's the *how* that really matters, and effective managers know they need to adapt their plans as they sail off to their goals. In their book built from decades of rich experience solving some of the biggest challenges we face, the authors present lively how-to steps to chart the path through problems to success. They also reinforce the motives that bring talented managers to tough problems: the instinct to wrestle with big issues to make a difference.

It's easy for cynics to believe that failure is inevitable. It's easy for Pollyannas to believe they can will problems away. It's the strong and effective leader who skillfully charts a course between these poles, the leader who keenly grasps the realities but uses a sense of mission to push through problems without being trapped in failures. For leaders who want to understand better how to do this, this book is an invaluable guide.

Donald F. Kettl
Dean
School of Public Policy
University of Maryland

ACKNOWLEDGMENTS

As the old saying goes, success has many fathers, but failure is an orphan. If that's the case, then it could follow that in writing a book about failure, we didn't have any help. That wasn't the case. Many people contributed, whether they know it or not—either by commenting on the work in progress or simply by the lessons we learned from them.

We benefited from the excellent current and earlier writings of numerous management and development theorists, including: Mark Bovens and Paul t'Hart, Karl Weick and Kathleen Sutcliffe, Edward Freeman, Rob Cross, David Krackhardt, Sue Conger, John Kotter, Nadim Matta, and Ron Ashkenas. Each helped shape our thinking as we developed the final five-rule model that underpins this book. These theorists are referenced within the text, and we learned much from reviewing their published works.

Significant contributions were made by peer reviewers: Don Kettle, Rosalia Rodriquez-Garcia, Vijayendra Rao, and Stephen Porter. Enough thanks can't be given to these very busy people who were each supportive and helpful.

Our World Bank colleagues David Wilson and Iris Semini, Joanna Watkins, Mike Trucano, and Mukesh Chawla were also generous with their suggestions and honest reviews of early drafts. We also benefited from the opinions offered by John Kusek, Robert Davidson, Robert Zall, John Novak, Tariqul Khan, Dora Cohenca, and Mohamed Khatori, who kindly acted as sounding boards for our ideas as they developed, even if they had to be convinced that project failure was a good topic for a book. Thank you Uma Balasubramanian and Mario Mendez for your unwavering support each time we asked for help in locating a reference or organizing important meetings.

We would also like to acknowledge and thank the participants from the 2012 IPDET program at Carlton University in Ottawa, Canada, who attended an early presentation on the Five Rule concept. We were provided with excellent suggestions on the book's framework and theory. Likewise, we thank the University of Witwaterstrand, in Johanesburg, South Africa, for their willingness to allow us to present the Five Rules to an audience of students and practitioners. We also thank the Government of the Free State, in South Africa, for allowing us to test early theories of the Five Rules on real problems encountered by the government.

Marelize Görgens would like to thank those who taught her to look beyond the process and to focus on analytical reasons for why things seldom happen the way they are planned on paper—most notably Jody Kusek and David Wilson, who mentored her in the early part of her career, as well as the countless governments at whose feet she learned how not to do development. Finally, Jody Kusek and Billy Hamilton would like to acknowledge the long, interesting spring and summer of 1993 that they spent working on Vice President Al Gore's National Performance Review. Working on reviews of all of the agencies of the federal government provided a lifetime supply of opinions on why some government programs work—and why others fail.

ABOUT THE AUTHORS

Jody Zall Kusek is an expert in results management and monitoring and evaluation (M&E). During her 13 years at the World Bank she has held both regional and corporate positions focusing on how the Bank can better align its resources and investments to achieve development results. She has worked in all six regions of the Bank and in over 30 countries. She is the co-author of *Ten Steps to a Results-Based Monitoring and Evaluation System*, now in its fifth printing and available in seven languages. This handbook is used by academic institutions, national governments, and development partners worldwide to better understand the principles and practices of results-based M&E. She also coauthored *Making Monitoring and Evaluation Systems Work*, published in June 2010. Earlier, Jody was a senior adviser and director in two cabinet agencies during the Clinton-Gore Administration in the United States, helping to design and implement the Government Performance and Results Act that is the hallmark of the U.S. strategic and program planning model.

Marelize Görgens Prestidge is a global development professional with 15 years of experience in program science, evaluation, and implementation research. She has helped governments analyze their development problems, implement solutions to improve service delivery, and evaluate their impact. Marelize has worked in the private sector, for nongovernmental organizations, and for the World Bank in the human development and agricultural sectors in executing analytical work, providing technical assistance, and building capacity in human development challenges through pragmatic solutions and evaluations.

Billy C. Hamilton is an expert in tax and fiscal policy and related issues. He authors a regular column on state tax issues for the national publication *State Tax Notes*. He currently is Interim Executive Vice President for Finance and Administration for the Capital Metropolitan Transportation Authority, serving on a part-time basis. Prior to January 2007, he was Chief Deputy Comptroller of Public Accounts of Texas. He has also served on special assignment as Co-Executive Director of the California Performance Review, for Governor Arnold Schwarzenegger, and as an assistant director of the National Performance Review under Vice President Al Gore in 1993. He was the first recipient (1998) of the Bullock Award for Public Stewardship and a fellow of the National Academy of Public Administration.

Introduction

We tend to seek easy, single-factor explanations of success. For most important things, though, success actually requires avoiding the many separate causes of failure. —Jared Diamond, American scientist and author

In early 2004, an international organization invested $50 million to help five Eastern European countries fight an HIV/AIDS epidemic—an epidemic driven largely by male and female sex work. The five governments agreed to be part of a regional program aimed at reducing the transmission of the HIV virus in the sex workers population. Initially, the regional program had huge support. Press conferences were held in each country announcing the effort.

Expectations were high. Yet in fundamental ways, the program was seriously flawed. The objectives were vague and unrealistic. Lines of authority over the individual country projects were unclear, and despite an early commitment from champions, there was little follow-up with important supporters and known critics once the program began. The countries were home to numbers of people with well-known cultural taboos about men having sex with men. Despite this, public broadcasts on the subject were put on the radio, on TV, and on roadway billboards across the five countries. The publicity angered important segments of the public almost from the beginning of implementation. Project team members were baffled at the unanticipated (but in hindsight, not surprising) resistance to getting the projects implemented.

The program was unable to establish clear management processes across the five countries. Due to this, procedures for hiring staff members were a nightmare to follow, and contractors often were not paid on time. Soon the work schedule began to slip. Despite the implementation challenges, the international organization and the country governments agreed to launch all aspects of the program simultaneously, without pilot testing to learn what worked and what did not. Eventually, the program failed.

This example is not an isolated occurrence. A recent performance review of the multilateral World Bank Group, undertaken by its Independent Evaluation Group, shows that almost a quarter of World Bank–funded projects and programs have failed.

Project failures are not confined to the development world. In 2004 Hartman and Ashrafi found that the project failure rate is above 60 percent for construction, engineering, and other technology projects, despite all the advances in project management theory and practice.

Failure is far from the minds or desires of either development partners or the developing-country governments, yet despite their efforts, failures persist. Why?

In some cases, the explanation lies in the difficulty of the interventions and the limitations of the governments involved. Many development projects touch on central aspects of society, including health, education, the private sector, and the treasury. At the same time, the international community is placing greater demands on those governments to "do more with less" and to show that results are being achieved with donor funds. The clashing demands can result in failure. Most government projects involve many processes, people, and stakeholders. Demands are high, but resources are limited. That failures happen should not surprise; it is amazing that any projects actually succeed.

What is project failure?

Failure and success are often thought of as alternative, binary conditions, but the dichotomy is misleading. For example, the collapse of a bridge is an event; that a bridge does not collapse is an ongoing state. *Failure*, in this sense, is the culmination of a series of events that led up to the collapse. Many avenues of failure are possible, but in most cases, one chain of events leads to failure. Thus, poor planning in the design of the bridge, substandard materials, and too much stress on the bridge at a particular moment cause the collapse. Some and perhaps most of those elements may have been present for a long time without a failure occurring. Some final element or elements are needed to trigger the collapse.

What, then, is project success? Numerous development organizations and project management experts, including the Project Management Institute, agree that project success can be defined as achievement of goals and objectives established at the beginning of the project. Many evaluation methods can be used to assess whether program goals have been achieved. Recently, development evaluation has encouraged the use of impact evaluation, a research-based method that relies on the use of control groups and other research techniques that were once within the domain of medical and social research.

However, knowing whether a project has succeeded or not is not the same as knowing when failure may or may not occur.

Mark Bovens and Paul 't Hart addressed this paradox in their examination of what they call "policy fiascoes." They offer a broad definition of a policy fiasco that seeks to encompass both the factual and the perceptual elements of a failure. A policy fiasco, they write, is "a negative event that is perceived by a socially and politically significant group of stakeholders in the community to be at least partially caused by avoidable and blameworthy failures of public policymakers" (1996, 15). Briefly, then, in a policy fiasco

- Something bad happens.
- Someone of sufficient political influence notices.
- The failure is publicized.
- Blame is assigned.

It is, in effect, a variation of the "six stages" of a project, cynically identified as enthusiasm, disillusionment, panic, search for the guilty, punishment of the innocent, and reward of the nonparticipant.

Project success and failure are not necessarily alternative states or extremes. Failure usually has a long lead time, culminating in a singular—somewhat disastrous—outcome. Hartman and Ashrafi (2004) wrote that projects do not often suffer from devastating failure. They do, however, have a propensity to run over budget; take longer to complete than was originally anticipated; or fail to deliver on expectations in terms of quality, scope, safety, or some other key stakeholder expectation.

In his book *Why Government Programs Fail*, James S. Larson (1980) defined failure broadly, as it applies to public programs, encompassing both the programmatic and the political nature of problems. "Failure," he wrote, "is any significant shortcoming in a government program that brings about subsequent changes in the law or in its implementation." Again, the triggering event (the shortcoming) and the political result (in Larson's definition, a policy response to the perceived failure) appear.

In the most general sense, failures can occur in three circumstances. First, something that is expected to happen does not happen. Second, something that was expected not to happen does happen. Third, something happens that was not considered at all. This simple division is useful, but it is not sufficient because it omits the element of control: What can a manager do, or what could he or she have done, to avoid the problem in the first place? In this regard, Bovens and 't Hart (1996) offer a typology of program failures that takes into account the idea of the controllability of failure. Their divisions are as follows:

- Foreseeable but controllable
- Foreseeable but uncontrollable
- Unforeseeable but controllable
- Unforeseeable but uncontrollable.

Their final category suggests the distinction that they make between mismanagement and misfortune—the recognition that some results are simply caused by, for lack of a better term, bad luck. Public managers are usually well aware that success or failure can turn on events outside their control. They can be taken by surprise by the same economic and natural events that surprise us all. "Man plans, and God laughs," as the old saying goes.

According to the World Bank, a recurring pattern of failure seems to persist in the aspects within the control of the project manager, such as poor objective setting, overambitious designs, weak results frameworks, and weak implementation capacity. However, factors outside the project's direct control, such as lack of government ownership and changes in government during implementation, are also named as culprits (IEG 2011). Elsewhere in the literature, technology, culture, content, and poor project management are cited as reasons for project failure in areas as varied as knowledge management (Chua and Lam 2005), construction (Iyer and Jha 2005), and agriculture (Kumar 2006). Hodgson and Cicmil, in their 2006 book *Making Projects Critical*, echoed the views of those investigators and summarized the reasons for project failure as "frequent cost overruns, delays, and underperformance in terms of quality and user satisfaction."

This book's interest, however, is in the very large percentage of projects not subject to events *beyond the control of project managers*. In this regard, attention to the possibility of failure is the best guarantee of success. Understandably, public managers may be uncomfortable with such an inherently negative approach to managing public projects, which are, after all, designed and intended to produce a public good or to solve a public problem. The point is not to be pessimistic but realistic in managing public projects. Anticipating and solving problems can avert compounding those problems and the failures that result.

Why study failure?

An obvious question now is, why focus on failure? Why not focus on success, which is the goal of all development programs? The simple answer is that many publications exist that celebrate innovation and tell upbeat stories of successful projects and encouraging results. Yet failure is common in public programs and is a major problem in development, where the obstacles are great and the potential for failure is great as well.

It is the authors' view that as much or more can be learned from considering why things go wrong as from examining why they go right. No two public policy programs unfold in the same way, but the elements that can cause them to fail or succeed often are common from one program to another. In its own way, failure provides a richer context for understanding why public programs work—and why they often do not. Studying those failures can increase the likelihood of success—by revealing that the line between success and failure is often very thin and difficult to discern until failure is imminent and possibly unavoidable.

In many public programs, moreover, success can be viewed as the absence of failure. As Fredrick Shiels (1991, 190) has pointed out, "We forget that the greatest success is often the absence of failure. The disaster averted is rarely recognized as such. Small prudent decisions that avoid a Chernobyl or a space shuttle tragedy almost by definition cannot be measured."

Finally, recognizing the sources of failure and preparing for them is a key step to managing the unexpected and building resilience into program design and execution. As Weick and Sutcliffe (2007) have written, "Whether we like it or not, if the world is filled with the unexpected, we're all firefighters putting out one fire after another" (163).

Address project failure head-on

When projects fail—whatever the apparent reason—the failure often can be traced to a lack of attention to the possibility of failure and how it arises. In *The Logic of Failure*, Dietrich Doerner points out that "failure does not strike like a bolt out of the blue; it develops gradually according to its own logic"

(1996, 10). Failures can result from many factors or combinations of factors. A short list of potential problems might include ill-defined development goals, poor planning, underestimated time requirements, inadequate resources, and ineffective monitoring and evaluation. Other factors when not addressed, early and throughout implementation, will create a project environment for failure. Such a situation typically occurs not because one thing goes wrong but because multiple, sometimes apparently innocuous problems fuse to create an environment ripe for failure.

Too often, when the unexpected occurs, managers of complex projects are unprepared. They do not see the problem coming, and when it arrives, they overreact, underreact, or choose the wrong strategy for dealing with it, often exacerbating the situation. Once problems escalate to the point of failure, a fix may or may not be possible, but the cost will be significant in money, time, and human resources.

Anticipate failure: Be a mindful manager

Why is the failure to prepare for the unexpected so commonplace? The answer is complicated, and various experts have offered explanations. Those explanations are not limited to development projects but are more generally related to the inherent difficulty of dealing with complex systems. People form fuzzy or ill-conceived goals. They do not manage stakeholder relations or pay enough attention to the process as it unfolds. They fail to recognize and correct errors as they occur. They do not learn from the past or from the experience of others. They are unwilling to change course when course change is vital.

This litany of difficulties does not mean that failure in complex programs is a forgone conclusion. People can learn how to deal with complex systems, how to recognize the precursors of failure and deal with them. They can, in short, learn to pay attention to the possibility of failure. University of Michigan professors Karl Weick and Kathleen Sutcliffe have called such attention to the possibility that the unexpected may occur "mindfulness." They contrast it with "mindlessness," a situation in which "people follow recipes, impose old categories to classify what they see, act with some rigidity, operate on automatic pilot, and mislabel unfamiliar new contexts as familiar old ones" (Weick and Sutcliffe 2007, 88). Mindlessness is not a lack of attention—or at least it is not that alone. Mindlessness is the absence of a predisposition to the idea that things can wrong—that failure is not just a possible outcome of a program, but can be the likely outcome, if project managers are not mindful of the risks of their undertaking and ready to respond to them.

The recognition and consciousness of failure are what mindful management is all about.

Mindlessness is not inevitable in development management. To borrow Weick and Sutcliffe's word, managers can become more mindful. The mindful manager is aware of the threat of program failure. The mindful manager is cognizant that failure is a potential result of any public undertaking. The mindful manager takes steps to avoid failure. Those steps begin at project inception and end when the project is completed.

To address project failure, many have turned to the field of project management. Since the 1950s, most of the work in project management has focused on addressing project scheduling problems, with the underlying assumption that addressing this "hard" (quantifiable and measurable) issue in relation to projects and project management would reduce project failures. Better schedules were meant to result in successful projects. Gantt charts, PERT (Program Evaluation and Review Technique), and CPM (Critical Path Method) analysis methods were all attempts to solve the delays, budget increases, scope creep, and quality problems that projects typically face. But addressing scheduling issues has not satisfactorily prevented projects from failing.

Development practitioners have learned this difficult lesson too. The very thing that development practitioners were trying to address—better project results—was getting further away from them because they were not anticipating failure. They were trying to control the hard elements associated with project failure without also focusing on the "soft," intangible reasons that contribute to projects' performing less than optimally and that are often—as the research into project failure shows—root causes of failure.

Our theory is built on the experience of failed projects and on the realization that although good design is essential, it is not enough. More than a good design determines the success or failure of a development project. Paying attention to details that only happen during implementation is essential in avoiding failure. Managers need to make a conscious commitment to imagining worst-case scenarios, to guarding against their occurrence, and to having a plan of action for the cases when they occur, despite all prior planning. Any project will face problems as it proceeds. Assumptions will not be borne out; players will change; even governments will change; and, most important, mistakes will be made. The key is to correct the problems as implementation progresses and prevent them from compounding into failure. Ironically, then, the path to successful development begins with understanding why programs fail.

Where do things go wrong?

In any project, many things potentially can go wrong. Inevitably, some things *will* go wrong. However, the project need not fail if the problems are recognized and dealt with before they begin to coalesce and cascade. In this regard, the first key to successful management is to recognize the precursors of failure. Because the sources of many project failures are related to implementation failures, we focus primarily on those.

We have come to the conclusion that four types of weaknesses can contribute to project failure: (a) poor alignment of design and implementation, (b) a weak enabling environment, (c) cases of ignoring red tape and bottlenecks, and (d) a failure to learn. As figure I.1 indicates, the categories can interact and combine to form a single pattern of failure.

One factor typically is not enough to ensure failure; rather, the accretion of problems—often across all the categories—produces the sequence that leads to failure.

Most of the precursors of implementation failure are recognizable to anyone who has participated in or managed a public reform program. Because those factors are often well known and recognized, one can reasonably ask why they are not more often intercepted in practice. Why are well-known risks to projects allowed to multiply, with few real strategies put in place to manage those risks? Many explanations are offered, particularly after a project fails. But the real explanation in many cases is that failure is "baked into" the project almost from the start by managers and team members who simply fail to be mindful of the details and who focus on avoiding the obvious problem spots that any project will face as it goes along (see table I.1).

The faults that allow the elements leading to project failure can take many forms. In some cases, managers and their organizations develop expecta-

Figure I.1 Interacting Sources of Project Failure

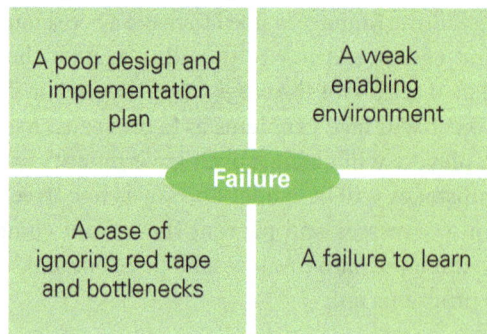

A poor design and implementation plan	A weak enabling environment
Failure	
A case of ignoring red tape and bottlenecks	A failure to learn

Table I.1 Program Failure Taxonomy

A poor design and implementation	A weak enabling environment	A case of ignoring red tape and bottlenecks	A failure to learn
• Vague and unclear goals	• Lack of senior management support	• Multiple bottlenecks in work processes	• Failure to admit mistakes
• Poor theory of change	• Not listening to project critics	• Process mapping not done for important activities	• Aversion to risk taking
• Theory of change unvalidated by evidence	• Poor communication inside and outside project	• Lack of delegation	• Launching project without piloting
• Lack of activity breakdown plan	• Poor management of political economy	• Rulebound	• No or wrong performance measures
• Poor communication	• Lack of stakeholder management plan to keep them informed and happy	• Poor communication up and down the work process	• Lack of time to incorporate learning into implementation plan
• No ownership over activity	• Poor understanding of informal environment		• Little feedback
• No measurable results	• Poor use of formal and informal networks		
• No implementation plan			
• Poor use of project resources			

tions for how a project should proceed, and those expectations produce a blind spot where a potential point of failure can fester and grow. In other cases, the manager may become distracted by one apparent problem and may focus on the wrong signal, thus allowing other problems to develop. In still other cases, inherent problems may be underestimated or undervalued even when they are recognized.

The causes of public policy failure are complex and multifaceted. At times, failure is unavoidable and uncontrollable, but we believe that more often it can be anticipated and controlled. Failure is not inevitable, but it is common.

To minimize the possibility of failure, we have come up with five rules for avoiding failure. We call this a "fail-safe" system because we not only plan for success but also anticipate the possibility of failure. Like a fail-safe system in the engineering world, our goal is to introduce strategies that will allow the project manager to anticipate points of failure and to have a plan for compensating for possible failure, if it does occur, in a way that causes the least possible disruption to the project. In this regard, we plan for failure so that we can achieve success. We believe that following a few simple rules can greatly increase the chances of success. Among those rules, the most important appear to be the following five:

1. Make it about the how. Asking the *why* and *what* questions can get the project objectives right and can make certain that the project is designed to achieve important results. However, asking the *how* questions helps to ensure that the project will be implemented to achieve results and at the lowest cost. This kind of successful implementation takes three things: (a) a clear statement and clear understanding of the methods and mechanisms used to deliver project outputs and the standards that will apply; (b) a detailed work and activity breakdown plan to implement according to those mechanisms and with the achievement of specific results in mind, at a given cost; and (c) the assignment of an activity owner, whose primary role is to make sure the activity is being implemented correctly, and who—when a problem occurs—has the authority to try to fix it while alerting the project managers.

2. Keep your champions close but your critics closer. Avoiding failure means understanding the importance of managing key stakeholders, both those in favor and those opposed to the effort. If senior management is not behind the effort, it likely will not succeed. Several studies—from Young and Jordan (2008), to Rondinelli (1993), and Bryde (2008), for example—have concurred that senior management support is essential for project success. Bryde (2008) went further to say that a project champion matters most, that such a project champion needs to have an internal and an external function, and that the managerial skills of project champions—not their technical prowess in a specific field—are most important. Senior management plays a game-changing role in determining project success or failure, irrespective of the organization involved. However, those not in favor of the project's moving forward, or the critics, can play just as important a role in whether or not the project fails. Failure to recognize the roles played both by people who have a positive view and those who have a negative viewpoint about project implementation will result in disaster.

3. Informal networks matter; work with them. Two types of organizations drive program implementation: formal and informal. Both are needed for projects to succeed. Projects that accomplish their goals know how to work "within the formal boxes" of organizational structure and the chain of command, as well as how to use the informal links or invisible networks across the organization. Avoiding failure means skillfully adapting to the realities and existence of the informal organization and allowing the team to make the best use of the various informal networks that can support a project's goals or can ensure that the work never gets done.

4. Unclog the pipes. Every project works through key processes, or each activity of a project has a stated process that allows work to move through it.

Projects that avoid failure anticipate possible bottlenecks that either slow work down or stop it altogether. By recognizing the potential for bottlenecks, the mindful manager is on the lookout for the possibility of those bottlenecks and removes them to avoid project failure.

5. Build the ship as it sails. Many if not most organizations do not establish management systems to learn from failure. Too often, government organizations have emphasized performance measurement for external reporting only, giving little attention to putting the performance information to use in internal management decision-making processes (Binnendijk 2000). Both Ayas (1996) and McShane and Wells (2004) confirm the notion that projects that lack a learning component and that do not adapt to changes in a structured manner do not often succeed.

This rule suggests that one not move too quickly when implementing a project design. Start on a smaller scale and pilot whenever possible. Some project activities, especially innovative aspects or activities never tried in a particular location, need to be tested to find out whether they will work. Projects that avoid failure are not afraid to make mistakes. This is how projects learn and improve.

This is what fail-safe management is about. Even if a project was soundly managed from a time, cost, scope, quality, and human resources and communications perspective, those five areas—if not acknowledged and managed—typically will make it fail. Projects fail for many reasons, and those five can be a starting place to look for the weaknesses.

In the following chapters of this guide, we present each rule along with simple tools to help determine whether a project needs to pay more attention to a particular weakness area. We have presented a number of real stories from real managers. However, as you might imagine, only a few brave souls were willing to present cases in which they failed to be mindful of the possibility of failure. Thus, we have created scenarios ourselves, amalgamated from the many stories of projects that failed. Finally, we offer a checklist that can be used to support a fail-safe approach to your project—or any other.

References

Ahsan, K., and I. Gunawan. 2010. "Analysis of Cost and Schedule Performance of International Development Projects." *International Journal of Management* 28 (1): 68–78.

Ayas, Karen. 1996. "Professional Project Management: A Shift toward Learning and a Knowledge Creating Structure." *International Journal of Project Management* 14 (3): 131–36.

Binnendijk, Annette. 2000. *Results-Based Management in the Development Co-operation Agencies: A Review of Experience; Background Report*. Paris: DAC Working Party on Aid Effectiveness, Organisation for Economic Co-operation and Development. http://www.oecd.org/development/evaluationofdevelopmentprogrammes/1886527.pdf.

Bovens, Mark, and Paul 't Hart. 1996. *Understanding Policy Fiascoes*. New Brunswick, NJ: Transaction Publishers.

Bryde, David. 2008. "Perceptions of the Impact of Project Sponsorship Practices on Project Success." *International Journal of Project Management* 26 (8): 800–09.

Chua, Alton, and Wing Lam. 2005. "Why KM Projects Fail: A Multi-Case Analysis." *Journal of Knowledge Management* 9 (3): 6–17.

Doerner, Dietrich. 1996. *The Logic of Failure: Recognizing and Avoiding Errors in Complex Situations*. New York: Metropolitan Books.

Hartman, Francis, and Rafi Ashrafi. 2004. "Development of the SMART™ Project Planning Framework." *International Journal of Project Management* 22: 499–510.

Hodgson, D., and S. Cicmil. 2006. *Making Projects Critical*. New York: Palgrave Macmillan.

IEG (Independent Evaluation Group). 2011. *IEG Annual Report 2011: Results and Performance of the World Bank Group*. Washington, DC: Independent Evaluation Group, World Bank Group.

Iyer, K. C., and K. N. Jha. 2005. "Factors Affecting Cost Performance: Evidence from Indian Construction Projects." *International Journal of Project Management* 23 (4): 283–95.

Kumar, Victoria. 2012. Presentation. Atlanta: Project Management Institute.

Larson, James S. 1980. *Why Government Programs Fail: Improving Policy Implementation*. New York: Praeger.

McShane, Thomas O., and Michael P. Wells, eds. 2004. *Getting Biodiversity Projects to Work: Toward More Effective Conservation and Development*. New York: Columbia University Press.

Rondinelli, Dennis A. 1993. *Development Projects as Policy Experiments*. 2nd ed. New York: Routledge.

Shiels, Frederick. 1991. *Preventable Disasters: Why Governments Fail*. Savage, MD: Rowman and Littlefield.

Weick, Karl E., and Kathleen M. Sutcliffe. 2007. *Managing the Unexpected*. 2nd ed. San Francisco: John Wiley and Sons.

Young, Raymond, and Ernst Jordan. 2008. "Top Management Support: Mantra or Necessity?" *International Journal of Project Management* 26 (7): 713–25.

RULE 1

Make it about the how

Vision without action is a daydream. Action without vision is a nightmare.
—Japanese proverb

Imagine you own a small construction company located in the capital of a small country in East Africa. The minister of housing and rural development has asked if you would help him build housing in remote areas of the country. Recruitment of qualified teachers to these areas has been difficult. Thus, the new government has promised that free housing would be available within six months if teachers agree to spend three years teaching in remote areas of the country. You agree to build 60 houses and are given preliminary funds to begin. You immediately develop an implementation plan, cost the project, and assess the material resources needed to complete the work. Your understanding is that the houses need to be built as soon as possible.

The minister mentioned that he hoped that some of the houses would be built in his home district. On the assumption that this was a directive, the implementation work plan scheduled several homes to be located in the minister's district. In fact, more than half of the houses were scheduled to be built there. Although the minister's district was an urban one, and teachers most often lived in their own homes while teaching, you still built half the houses there. The project did not fund other activities, such as a promotion and advertising campaign to tell rural communities how to request the new housing, so no teachers applied during the recruitment period. The housing project was also not linked to other available incentives, such as rural allowances for teachers.

The teaching service commission did not know about the housing scheme as it placed teachers in specific schools. This resulted in homes being built but few teachers agreeing to live in them. Also, the project turned out to have enough funds for only 50 homes. To produce the 60 promised, corners were cut, and several of the houses used cheaper materials that were low in quality.

The result was that most of the houses were never occupied, and the few teachers who would live in them complained of being seen as special friends of the minister. The houses were built, but this project failed.

If you don't know where you are going, ask the right questions

The fact that this project failed came as quite a surprise to your company. You completed your goal of building 60 houses, on time and within the budget given. As far as the location of the new houses, there never was a clear project directive about where to build them. In fact, it was not clear that building the 60 homes would actually help recruit qualified teachers to rural areas. The goal of the education ministry, which was to increase the number of rural children with access to quality education, was not communicated. Moreover, the minister did not make known the overall objectives of the effort. Both parties made many assumptions without checking with the other partner as to their validity. They had different ideas of what the project intended to achieve. Your understanding was that the project's goal was to build 60 houses as soon as possible, with many located in the district of the minister. The minister's idea was to build political credibility to fulfill his election promises. In addition, a key group of stakeholders, teachers, understood that the project was to provide additional allowances over and above housing to entice them to work in rural areas. You failed to ask yourself the obvious: Why are we building 60 houses? What is the greater purpose of the houses, and how can the way in which I plan the house-building process further the broader goal of increasing access to quality rural education?

An important reason why many rural children were not in school was that few qualified teachers were willing to take up posts in rural provinces without suitable living arrangements and without accompanying allowances to compensate them for the inconvenience of living in a rural area. How is it possible that the minister, the teachers, and the contractor could understand the project objectives so completely differently? The minister eventually was sacked over this scandal, and your company's reputation was in ruins.

Fail-safe management starts by getting the why and what right

In the preceding scenario, some important questions were never asked by those implementing the program. Nor were they articulated by those who conceived the program. For example, Why are the houses needed? What activities need to be implemented to support the project goal? Why are certain houses being built in this district rather than that one? What needs to be included in the project documents to make sure the houses are livable for the teachers? In fact, had such questions been asked, the disaster described might never have happened. Asking these *why* and *what* questions can help the project become "results focused."

Kusek and Rist, in their 2004 book *Ten Steps to a Results-Based Monitoring and Evaluation System,* discussed the results movement taking hold in the area of public sector management. This movement involved shifting away from traditional project management approaches that focused on the project activities, budgets, and disbursements (as in the example above) toward new, results-based approaches that began to ask, What does success look like from all perspectives and to choose activities to achieve that. At that time, governments and other organizations around the world were grappling with internal and external demands for improvements in how public funds are managed. New pressure came from a global economy that eschewed government waste and called on development to "do more with less." This pressure was coming from seemingly everywhere: development partners, parliaments, citizens groups, the private sector, and nongovernmental organizations.

The clamor for greater accountability and better government quickly found its way to developing countries where the state had often failed to deliver even fundamental public goods such as property rights, roads, basic health, and education. Stakeholders were no longer solely interested in the activities of government but wanted to know what those activities were producing for a larger society. How were government-funded activities achieving promises made to citizens for better delivery of services?

This new focus on results was an important impetus to ask questions in a new way: Why are we investing in this project? What is the objective of the project relative to the problem? What would success look like at the end of the project? What performance measures, when tracked on a regular basis, would help assess whether the project is making progress? In summary, are development initiatives making a difference to people on the ground?

A decade ago, this focus was a sea change from the traditional way that projects were designed and planned. For example, we no longer assume that building new hospitals is always linked to improvement in a person's health. Results-based thinking allows decision makers to rethink which projects will be funded and which ones will not, and, most important, *how* projects will be implemented. With fewer resources available and more competition for those resources, a focus on results calls for funding the right projects to help solve real problems that people care about.

No one would disagree that over the past decade, results-based management has been a welcome approach to managing development projects. In fact, over the past decade hundreds of books, papers, courses, and policies have been published about how to design a results-based project and how to "manage to results." We have also supported this movement through our writings and teaching.

Figure 1.1 is an example of how "results-oriented" thinking was used to design the *what* in a health project. To reduce maternal mortality, the project team identified three interventions: (a) increased adoption of prevention methods, (b) increased use of maternal health services, and (c) improved access to family planning. The project team further identified *what* activities

Figure 1.1 **Example: Health Sector**

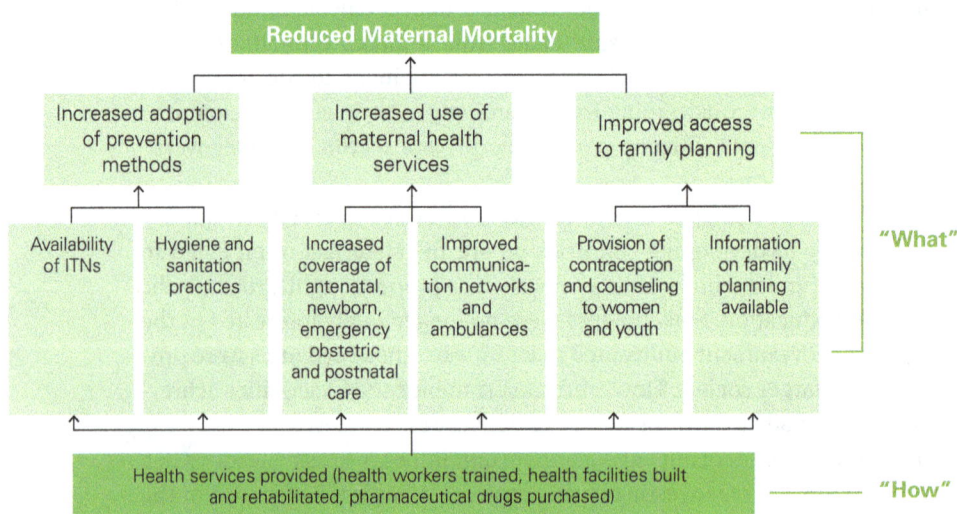

Source: World Bank, 2008

would need to be implemented to achieve the project goal. Asking a series of *what* questions, such as what would success look like and what needs to be done to achieve this, is referred to as the "logic" of the project.

While a logic exercise is useful to make certain the project is sensibly designed, it is not particularly helpful to answer the *how* questions: How will the health workers be trained? How will the health facility be built? How are the pharmaceutical drugs purchased?

A detailed work plan is needed to translate the *whats* into specific activities to be implemented. Focusing on the *how* is as important as the *why* and *what*. Vijayendra Rao, a leading economist at the World Bank, writes that it is project implementation—which can consume up to 90 percent of project costs—that deserves urgent attention (Rao 2012). Dr. Rao also believes that poor implementation can be the weakest link in aid effectiveness. To be failsafe, project teams need to think about the possible things that can go wrong during implementation and include them in the project plan. Figure 1.2 shows how the *how* can be linked to the *what* in a results planning model.

Make it about the how

In every project work plan, activities are further broken down into tasks. A "work breakdown tool" can be used to help manage the tasks. The following steps describe how to use the tool to manage project tasks (see also figure 1.3).

1. Break the activity down, showing its final deliverable and subdeliverables.
2. For key deliverables, the work process steps should be mapped to look for ways to streamline or to identify possible barriers or bottlenecks that

Figure 1.2 Linking Implementation Planning to Results Planning

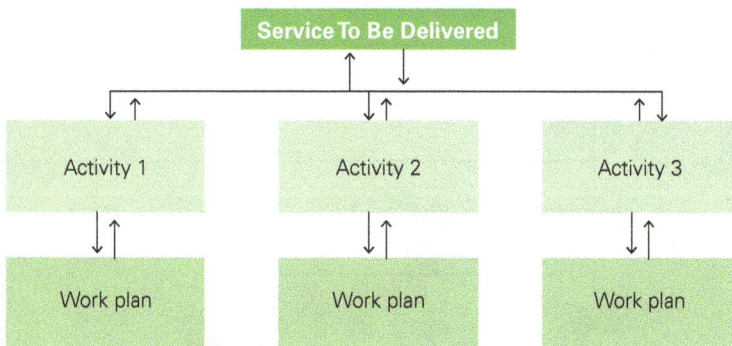

Source: Based on Net MBA.com

would need to be addressed to make sure that the work can flow through the process. The tasks should be understandable, so that an estimate of resources needed is outlined and costed with confidence.

3. When tasks or resource levels are unknown, those elements should be identified and implemented first. This approach allows for unknowns to be investigated further and for action to be taken to resolve them.

4. The project manager should assign an activity task manager. This person has authority to "own" the activity and has accountability to make sure that implementation occurs.

5. The project manager needs to hold regular meetings with activity leaders to discuss all issues involving the project's implementation and to catch and resolve problems early.

Note that Task 2 of the work breakdown plan calls for mapping the task work process. This mapping shows where activities can be streamlined or where bottlenecks can occur that will slow or stop the work from moving through the process. We rarely find teams that take the time to do this mapping, yet bottlenecks can result in failed efforts. Rule 4—Unclog the pipes—specifically addresses this problem.

Forgetting the how can lead to failure

In the scenario described earlier in this chapter, failure to plan or implement key work tasks contributed to the failure of the housing project. An imple-

Figure 1.3 **Task Breakdown Structure**

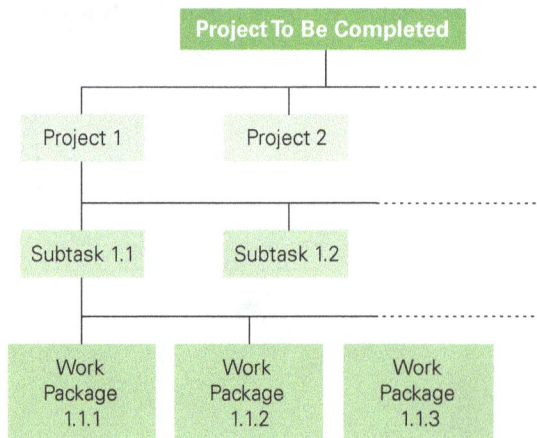

mentation plan of sorts existed, but the project manager failed to budget key tasks and thus ran out of funds before all 60 homes were built. Moreover, the minister and his team failed to plan for other key activities, such as teacher recruitment. That omission contributed to a poor alignment of the project's goal of getting qualified teachers hired and located in rural areas, with the task of building the houses and making them available.

Recently, on assignment to South Africa, we met with a number of government officials who shared their concerns about not knowing how to implement a project to achieve results. They stressed that although much emphasis was being placed on designing projects to achieve results, they were at a loss as to just how to get the project done. Each official had been trained by international experts in results-based management, and all regularly used its tools, such as results chains, project indicators, scorecards, and results frameworks. Nevertheless, they believed that their organization was no longer paying the necessary attention to *how* to move forward in managing the work. How do they take available resources and develop an implementation plan to begin to get the job done?

The government officials felt that so much emphasis had been placed on asking the *why* and *what* questions that they no longer knew where to get their many *how* questions answered:

- How do we mobilize the needed resources?
- How do we develop a plan to deliver the intended activities of this project?
- How do we cost each activity to ensure that we budget enough money for the entire activity?
- How do we ensure compliance in each aspect of the project?
- How should services be implemented most efficiently, to save costs without compromising quality and to increase the numbers of people who are reached?
- How do we deliver the results needed, on time and within budget, to everyone who needs them, at lowest cost?

In Swaziland, a country neighboring South Africa, the government made a bold decision not to revise a strategic plan, as is customary after five years, but rather to focus exclusively on the *how* and develop implementation guidelines. The government decided to go in that direction because the current strategy goals, short- and medium-term results were still relevant to the development issue at hand. However, they were not being achieved as expected. Thus, instead of taking a traditional approach of rewriting an already excellent strategy, the government opted to (a) set even more challenging new targets and then (b) develop a rigorous national implementation and scale-up strategy for key government services and make certain that the country was using least-cost methods to reach the new targets. For each of the services identified in its strategy, Swaziland proceeded to develop national implementation guidelines (like standard operating procedures). It also established much closer supervision of how the targets for each organization would be implemented.

We spoke with a number of teams of failed projects and heard similar tales about the lack of emphasis on just getting the job done. One concern was that often, during regularly scheduled project reviews, a long list of performance indicators was reviewed as the basis for whether or not the project was on track. However, performance indicators are meant to present data on where a project is at a single moment in time. If for some reason the indicator showed that the project was not advancing as planned, it was impossible to determine where the problem was and the degree of seriousness.

In summary, although the tools introduced through results-based management are important, they need to be augmented by other tools that help managers and teams manage the work itself. Both are important. Asking the *why* and *what* questions can get the project objectives right and can make certain that the project is designed to achieve the desired results. Asking the *how* questions helps ensure that the project will be implemented for the lowest cost when the results are achieved. Good implementation is based on four principles: (a) a clear statement of which products and services will be delivered and how deliverables are aligned to a larger goal; (b) articulation of the methods and mechanisms through which products and services will be delivered; (c) a detailed work plan and an activity breakdown plan to implement each activity, at a given cost, with achievement of the larger project goals or results in mind; and (d) assignment of an activity owner whose primary role is to make sure the activity is being implemented correctly and who, when a problem occurs, has the authority to try to fix it while alerting the project managers. The organization must be committed to fixing problems, not assigning blame.

Every ship needs a captain. Every project needs to make sure that someone has the job of ensuring that every key activity is implemented as planned. Ensuring that one individual is both responsible and accountable for implementing key parts of the project may mean that it may actually get done.

References

Kerzner, H. 2009. *Project Management: A Systems Approach to Planning, Scheduling, and Controlling*. Hoboken, NJ: John Wiley and Sons.

Kusek, Jody Zall, and Ray C. Rist. 2004. *Ten Steps to a Results-Based Monitoring and Evaluation System*. Washington, DC: World Bank.

Rao, Vijayendra. 2012. "With Foreign Aid, Failure Is Essential to Learning." *Toronto Globe and Mail*. www.theglobeandmail.com. January 23, 2012.

Make it about the how

Build the safe bet first

Keep your champions close but your critics closer

Fail-Safe

Unclog the pipes

Informal networks matter— work with them

RULE 2

Keep your champions close but your critics closer

Your most unhappy customers are your greatest source of learning.

—Bill Gates

Imagine this: You are deputy minister of education in a large Middle Eastern country where 50 percent of citizens are under 18 years of age. You are proud that so many students are in the secondary education system, but a continuing problem has been to acquire up-to-date science textbooks for thousands of students across the country. When schools finally have the correct number of books, the material is out of date. The Gates Foundation and Google[1] ask if your country is interested in participating in a new project that will provide children with smartphones and age-appropriate digital science applications. The project will involve purchasing 100,000 low-cost smartphones. Google's search engine and access will be made available without charge. The only cost to the country will be for the use of the local telecommunication connections. The project also includes a component to provide teachers with the same materials as the students, but with additional applications dedicated to science curriculum and teaching tools. A similar project elsewhere in the region resulted in increases in science test scores from an average pass rate of 45 percent to more than 80 percent.

The president, the parliament, and the private sector were excited about the project and offered support as needed. Part of the scheme would be that local phone stores would supply the phones paid for by the project. As a result of this venture, revenues from phone sales increased for those small businesses that were part of the program. Likewise, teachers and students were so excited to be part of the initial group of participating schools that attendance at those schools increased by more than 25 percent.

Unfortunately, two groups came forward to oppose the project. These were clergy members and groups of highly religious parents. These groups were concerned that the children would use the phones to connect to "undesirable" social media outlets. They felt that their way of life was threatened by their young children's exposure to objectionable cultural practices. Many children's parents refused to allow them to participate or to have the phones. The project failed.

Stakeholders matter

Edward Freeman's 1984 book *Strategic Management: A Stakeholder Approach* is widely credited with introducing the term "stakeholders" into modern management theory. He defined a stakeholder as any group or individual who can affect or be affected by a company's purpose. Luiz Rocha, in his paper "Intimacy and Quills," said, "In every undertaking, there are parties with a vested interest in the activities and results of the project. These parties are called *stakeholders:* individuals with some kind of stake, claim, share, or interest in the activities and results of the project" (2010, 6).

In projects, stakeholders are often viewed as a source of risk with unclear motives. Therefore, it is important to pay close attention to groups in favor of the project and those highly critical of it. Stakeholder consultation is typically part of most new development projects. Town hall meetings and other forums are often held with individuals and groups who want to know the possible negative or positive role the project will have for them. If consultations are held early enough, project designs are even changed to accommodate issues brought up by stakeholders. Still, it is not uncommon for consultations to be vague as to their purpose, with invitees a collection of representatives from government and interest groups, along with ordinary citizens.

Over the past 30 years, numerous management theorists and economists have embraced a school of thinking on the importance of who is included in the consultations, as well as the role of certain groups relative to others. How to determine which group holds the most power is an important part of this thinking. The theory behind knowing "where the power lies" assumes that stakeholders with the most power will have the most influence over the success or failure of the program or project and thus will need to be most carefully managed.

In the case of Colombia's displaced people, described in box 2.1, the government failed to take into account the power of strong NGOs and other

---

BOX 2.1

Colombia's Displaced People Had Champions

Decades of insurgent warfare and violence by drug cartels displaced millions of Colombians from their homes. Some fled across borders into Ecuador, Panama, and República Bolivariana de Venezuela. Most crowded into Bogotá or other large cities. The majority of the victims were rural subsistence farmers or members of indigenous groups and ethnic minorities, with little political, social, or economic influence. Government efforts to help them were uneven and were hindered by turbulent politics and inadequate public resources. The displaced may have been in plain sight, but they were virtually invisible.

Nongovernmental and international aid organizations never lost sight of the growing population, however, and along with civil society and faith-based groups, kept their dreadful circumstances on Colombia's development agenda. Public pressure mounted, and the government, sometimes reluctantly, issued decrees requiring a comprehensive plan to address the problem. The courts joined in and imposed rulings favoring the restoration of property and rights to individual victims. But implementation lagged, and the numbers kept building—up to as many as 5 million displaced persons.

As years passed, the community of external champions demanding action grew and included opposition politicians, academics, and citizens associations. They used the media, the courts, public hearings, and election politics to keep up the pressure. It worked. The national legislature eventually passed a law declaring "unconstitutional" the state of Colombia's displaced citizens and demanding that the government report regularly about financial and other support dedicated to correcting the problem. Resources began flowing more regularly; public bureaucracies improved; and new organizations emerged to partner with the government at the national, state, and local levels. Awareness, collaboration, and a commitment to problem solving began to replace mere formal compliance.

Today, services remain uneven, and mostly poor people continue to be displaced by violence. The cycle likely will repeat itself until armed groups and the government reach a lasting accord. But now, the least powerful of Colombia's citizens are no longer simply ignored, invisible, or disenfranchised by their government. Instead, they are at the center of a well-funded, increasingly capable effort to find permanent and dignified solutions to their displacement. Progress has been slow, but it is picking up speed, a trajectory that would not have been possible without the sustained involvement of a wide variety of public, private, national, and international actors. Colombia's promising new public policy would not have been implemented without the persistent efforts of external champions and their constant support of Colombia's displaced citizens.

Source: Robert Davidson, U.S. government, 2012.

---

interest groups to influence public policy on the growing population displaced by decades of insurgent warfare and violence by drug cartels. As we learn from the Colombia story, stakeholders matter. Government officials, project managers, and other decision makers do not always understand their influence and ability to affect policy or project implementation. Failure to recognize and carefully manage relationships with those people who have a positive or a negative reaction to a project or policy can result in disaster.

Research by Legris and Collerette (2006) showed that a high project failure rate can be attributed to a lack of attention to stakeholders. Olander and Landin (2005) write that stakeholders' negative attitudes toward a project can cause cost overruns and time delays because of conflicts over both design and implementation. Some stakeholder groups might try to limit or cancel a project altogether. Mitchell, Agle, and Wood (1997) offer that the concerns of stakeholders who have greater power, legitimacy, and urgency will be given the greatest priority.

Mindful managers seek out champions

There is no single, accepted method to assess the role of stakeholders in the project environment. Several management experts have proposed methods that are simple and helpful. Lynda M. Applegate of Harvard University provides a step-by-step approach that involves (a) defining project issues and cross-listing each individual, group, unit, or organization that has a stake in success or failure; (b) typing those by whether they are champions or critics; (c) rating the importance of each to the success of the project; and (d) finally identifying actions necessary to meet, clarify, or realign stakeholder interests and expectations (Applegate 2008).

Experts from construction engineering have also written extensively about the importance of knowing the roles of various stakeholders in project environments. In their 2009 book *Construction Stakeholder Management*, Chinyio and Olomolaiye developed a simple grid to help project teams manage the complicated relations of those in favor of and those opposed to large construction projects. Their grid is a two-by-two matrix that places the level of interest of various stakeholders on one axis and their relative power on the other. They believe that while keeping stakeholders in a "happy state" is acceptable for those with significant power but little interest in the project, it is imperative to manage powerful stakeholders with significant interest in the project (figure 2.1). Regardless of whether the stakeholder is a champion or a critic, these relationships must be managed to avoid project failure.

Figure 2.1 A Power–Interest Matrix

Interest

LOW   HIGH

Power	HIGH	Maintain these stakeholders in a happy state	Manage these stakeholders closely
		Keep an eye on these stakeholders and act when prompted	Keep these stakeholders happy and informed
	LOW		

Source: Chinyio & Olomolaiye (2010: 89)

Source: Chinyio and Olomolaiye 2009, 89.

Alex Laufer wrote in *Breaking the Code* that "many program managers, unfortunately, tend to communicate with champions and other stakeholders only in the early stages of the program, when they must seek their input in order to formulate the program's requirements." Thus, "they might not seek input again until a crisis erupts" (Laufer 2009).

Stakeholder positions often change over the project life cycle and should be assessed regularly throughout implementation. Being realistic about why different groups support or oppose the project is important. If the underlying reasons of those in favor of and against the program are not known, managing those relationships over the life of a project will be difficult.

Manage stakeholder groups according to their ability to affect the project's success or failure

Champions are a particular type of stakeholder who may have identified a need for change in a particular area and are committed to making that change happen (Mind Tools 2012). Within the organization, a champion is typically a person who is part of senior management or who is close to the inner leadership circle. A champion has the authority and influence within the organization to ensure that the project has the support necessary to be successful. Without a project champion, a project will fail.

Mind Tools has proposed six characteristics of a good champion:

- Having sufficient influence within the organization to defend its cause
- Understanding, or being involved in developing, the organization's over-all strategy and being able to speak about how the project objectives help achieve the strategy
- Having the authority to make final decisions
- Having a vested interest in the project's outcomes
- Being able to represent the project in solving problems involving different stakeholders
- Being able to communicate effectively with all levels of the organization (Mind Tools 2012).

Champions are essential, regardless of the nature of the project. The Project Management Institute, in Washington, D.C., suggests that the very first step of project planning is the identification of a project champion. This person is not necessarily an individual involved in the project on a day-to-day basis or the project manager. Instead, a champion is a person who intimately understands the "big picture" results that the project wants to achieve and has the interests of the project at heart.

Champions may be motivated by a sense of public responsibility with regard to a particular development issue. They may also be motivated by a desire for personal gain and political recognition within the institutions of government that are important to them. Taking on the role of public champion is always a political risk, given that political winds keep blowing in different directions over the life of a program.

Critics also have their reasons for being against a project. Difference in ideology is one reason. Such opponents, often called "counterreformers," may simply believe that government should be heading in a different direction. Or they might be endorsing a different project with similar or competing goals. Sometimes critics have a personal agenda that is in conflict with the project. They may believe that the project will lessen their authority, clout, or position in government or other institutions in the country.

Manage relations with champions and opponents as a key project activity

Mapping out power relations is only the first step. Asking *why* powerful stakeholders hold a particular position is important to the ability to manage relationships so that stakeholders continue to support the program, or at least do not create problems.

Stakeholder mapping is done at the concept phase of a project, repeated at the start of implementation, and revisited at the beginning of each funding year. Although champions and critics may already be known, learning their motives is crucial to prevent the program from being blindsided with negative publicity or, worse, having a counter-reformer with the power to undermine the team's efforts.

In the story "Ever Wonder Where Protein Drinks Come From?" (box 2.2), the project team neglected to map relations and nearly neglected one of its most important stakeholders, the regulatory authority.

Too often, once the relationships are analyzed, one team member is given the role of maintaining contact with the champions and other stakeholders. That team member will be responsible if the relationship is troubled or needs repair. They will alert decision makers when problems occur with the relationship and inform the team about potential issues with critics.

In some program environments, maintaining those relationships is not even within the program team's control but is a higher-level function of the government. The program might be one among many with similar stakeholders. Sometimes only a few select individuals are authorized to interact with the powerful individuals.

We think that everyone on the project team should be expected at one time or another to manage the champion and other stakeholder relationships, through regular and frequent meetings in which the entire program team briefs the champion or through one-on-one meetings to discuss specific issues that need the continuing support of project champions.

In the story at the beginning of this chapter, the most powerful champion for the project was the country's president. He saw opportunity on several levels: producing new income for small businesses, solving the problem of providing up-to-date science information for the children in his country, and possibly increasing international competitiveness. However, he failed to take into account the powerful voice of the clergy. Although his country was moving toward secularism, the clergy maintained a strong role as the cultural mainstay of many families.

The tool in table 2.1 has been adapted from a number of tools found in the literature on managing stakeholder relations. We also offer a few steps for using it:

- List key stakeholders who are likely to influence the project. This list should be reviewed at least quarterly.
- Update your power-mapping grid every few months during implementation.

- Formally meet with the entire team to agree on what is needed from each stakeholder.
- Assign responsibility for managing a particular stakeholder.
- Formulate messages and stick to them; do not make up messages as you go along.

BOX 2.2

Ever Wonder Where Protein Drinks Come From?

More than 40 years ago, a marketing representative for a U.S. company known for its industrial machinery and the director of research, development, and production of a well-known dairy product manufacturing company located in New York State had an idea. What if ultrafiltration and reverse osmosis membrane technology could be applied to the cheese industry? At the time, membrane equipment was used to desalinate seawater and was never used to support the food industry. Also at that time, during cheese manufacturing, the whey protein was thrown away as part of the manufacturing process. What if membranes could help capture the proteins before they were sent to the sewer and the industry could use them to develop a whole host of new dairy products or to enrich the ones currently on the market? Like any new idea, this one would take money, a champion, and a plan.

The two innovators sketched out a plan for how to test and possibly scale up the new venture. First, they knew that their idea might, in time, revolutionize cheese making, and thus they knew they had better figure out who their supporters and detractors would be. With this information in hand, they briefed key decision makers within the two companies on both the likely new revenues and the costs of testing whether their idea would work. After more analysis and more planning, the two companies agreed to fund a small-project incubator to test the concept. To the amazement of even the most skeptical, a host of new products were soon moving through the assembly line, including a dried protein powder that could be used for many products.

However, the team, in its excitement, forgot to bring along the New York State Department of Environment and Health. This regulatory agency was tasked to certify if new food products were fit for human consumption. In the United States, manufacturing processes must be certified to ensure that products met quality standards. The team forgot this important stakeholder. In fact, this stakeholder turned out to be the biggest skeptic. Due to its current restricted use, no one had yet presented data on the role of ultrafiltration in food processing.

Once the concerns of the regulators were known, the project team decided that it would seek the help of some of the most well-respected dairy experts in the world to help prove to the regulatory agency that the protein powder was indeed safe. Further tests were undertaken, more analyses were performed, and—over time—the manufacturing process was approved for food use.

Over the many years since this work began, many other international and national companies have further innovated the manufacturing processes and have patented many other uses of the product. The young innovators of 40 years ago almost lost their opportunity to contribute to a billion dollar industry because they missed managing one of their most important stakeholders. They never forgot this lesson.

Source: Robert. R. Zall, Professor Emeritus, Cornell University, personal communication.

Table 2.1 Tool for Managing Stakeholder Relations

Stakeholder name	Key interests and issues	Power status	Level of support	Project team contact	Actions desired (if any)	Agreed messages	Action and follow-up

Ask these key questions when using Rule 2

- Who is the project's champion?
- What is motivating the stakeholders?
- Have key stakeholders been identified?
- Has power mapping been done?
- What is the plan for managing key stakeholder relations?
- How often has the plan been reviewed and updated?
- Have problems in key relationships been brought to the attention of the champion?
- What more needs to be done to improve relationships at various project phases?

Note

1. This is a made-up case, not real. The companies mentioned have never provided such a scheme, nor to our knowledge do they plan to do so.

References

Applegate, Lynda M. 2008. "Stakeholder Analysis Tool." Harvard Business School Exercise 808–161. May.

Chinyio, Ezekiel, and Paul Olomolaiye. 2009. *Construction Stakeholder Management*. Oxford, U.K.: John Wiley and Sons.

Freeman, Edward. 1984. *Strategic Management: A Stakeholder Approach*. Boston: Pitman.

Laufer, Alexander. 2009. *Breaking the Code of Project Management*. New York: Palgrave Macmillan.

Legris, Paul, and Pierre Collerette. 2006. "A Roadmap for IT Project Implementation: Integrating Stakeholders and Change Management Issues." *Project Management Journal* 37 (5): 64–75.

Mind Tools, Project Management. 2012. "Building Support for Your Projects." http://www.mindtools.com/pages/main/newMN_PPM.htm#Support.

Mitchell, Ronald, Bradley Agle, and Donna Wood. 1997. "Toward a Theory of Stakeholder Identification and Salience: Defining the Principle of Who and What Really Counts." *Academy of Management Review* 22 (4): 853–86.

Olander, Stefan, and Anne Landin. 2005. "Evaluation of Stakeholder Influence in the Implementation of Construction Projects." *International Journal of Project Management* (23): 321–28.

Rocha, Luiz. 2010. "Intimacy and Quills: The Challenges of Managing by Projects." Paper presented at the 24th International Project Management Association World Congress, Istanbul, Turkey, November 1–3.

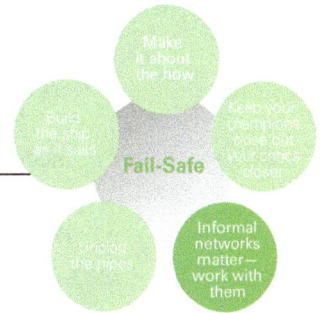

Make
it about
the how

Build
the ship
as it sail

Keep your
champions
close but
your critics
closer

Fail-Safe

Unclog
the pipes

Informal
networks
matter—
work with
them

RULE 3

Informal networks matter— work with them

If the formal organization is the skeleton of a company, the informal is the central nervous system driving the collective thought processes, actions, and reactions of its units.—David Krackhart and Jeff Hanson

A populous country in Asia recently elected its president for a second term in a fully democratic process. In his first term, the president appointed a blue ribbon panel to develop recommendations for a four-year plan of government reform. The panel included technical experts on governance, as well as respected community leaders and representatives from major national stakeholder groups. The panel reviewed thousands of pages of documents, interviewed hundreds of individuals, and established South-South learning workshops to understand similar reforms undertaken by other Asian countries. After three months, the chair of the panel, a noted professor from the country's top university, presented the panel's recommendations to the government.

The plan identified several disturbing governance issues. Only 9 percent of citizens trusted the government to deliver on promises made by leaders. Key public services were considered abysmal. Students in rural areas often lacked qualified teachers, and citizens reported less-than-adequate access to maternal health services. Most important, citizens were demanding more transparency in how government posts were filled and an end to cronyism in hiring. The president promised that if reelected he would improve the delivery of important services and address other issues of concern to citizens.

The plan was accepted by the president, and the panel disbanded. The media ran positive stories in local newspapers and on the radio about the success of the undertaking. Citizens were excited and, not surprisingly, the president was reelected.

One year later (five months after the reelection of the president), key department managers complained that their attempts to implement the reforms were being stalled, despite significant support from key champions. An international consulting firm was hired to determine why so little progress was being made. Its review identified a number of issues, but most relevant appeared to be the unexpected pushback from a number of informal networks within the agencies tasked to implement the reforms.

The consulting group pointed out that when new formal organization charts were drawn, they failed to take into consideration how work was successfully being implemented in parts of the government. It appeared that success was related to the informal role of a number of individuals who were both trusted and needed for their technical expertise. It seemed that with the new formal charts, many of those people were no longer easily able to provide critical input toward the reform effort. Formal organization charts are important because they lay out new program reporting relationships, new service rules and guidelines, and even new service standards. However, the new charts were also barriers to old communication networks, which resulted in reduced trust in the work environment. The roles of existing and necessary relationships were neither understood nor effectively used to support the success of reform.

Be aware of both formal and informal network structures

Every organization has two channels of communication within it: formal and informal. Although the formal organizational structure describes the lines of authority, much of the influence, information sharing, and work takes place through an informal structure that relies on existing relationships, contacts, and lines of communication.

Informal networks have a potentially enormous effect on the success or failure of projects, yet their value to the organization is often ignored because of lack of understanding of how to use them. They are seldom considered during the design of formal organizations, but ignoring them—or having dysfunctional informal networks—is a recipe for program failure.

Why formal structures?

Formal structures are needed to help classify the organization into parts. Formal organizations indicate who is in charge, who reports to whom, and what relationships exist between the various work elements. As mentioned earlier, they also are responsible for standard setting and for establishing norms and values for the rest of the organization.

For example, the World Health Organization provides countries with written standards and guidelines for the safe manufacturing and quality of vaccines for children. The standards provide assurance that every child vaccinated in Tanzania, for example, will have the same protection as a child vaccinated in Vietnam. Certainly not all health care providers in those countries are aware, or care, that in Geneva, Switzerland, a formal organization exists to establish coordination and authority over how vaccines are made and distributed. Yet we need the formal organizations to keep us from possible harm and to provide quality standards for goods and services.

Types of organizational structures

In the figures below, we present four typical organization designs: (a) traditional hierarchy, (b) team-based structure, (c) matrix, and (d) hybrids that incorporate more than one structure (Görgens and Kusek 2009).

An organization should choose the type of structure that best suits its needs. This will depend on a variety of things; for example, the structure can be based on geographical regions, products, or hierarchy.

Traditional structures are based on functional divisions and departments. These kinds of structures tend to have clear rules and procedures with precise authority lines for all levels. Subtypes of traditional organizational structures include:

Line structure. This kind of structure has a very specific line of command. Approvals and orders originate from top to bottom in a line, hence the name line structure.

Figure 3.1 represents a line structure or hierarchical organization. In this example, the vice president is the most powerful person in the organization, with the director the next most powerful, and so on. Decision making would

Figure 3.1 Line Structure Organizational Model

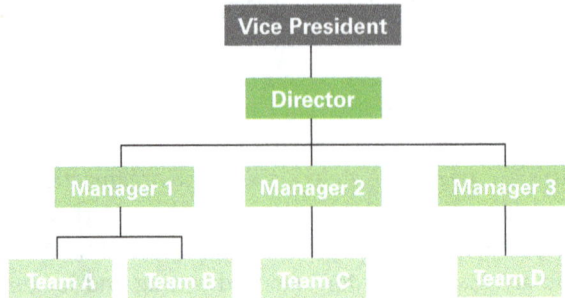

flow up and down this particular organization from the most powerful to the least powerful, and technical or other professional work would be done by those closer to the bottom of the hierarchy. The chart also presents a model that shows how communication is likely to flow.

Other formal structures are often used in organizations. Structures are usually designed to fit the needs of a particular organization. In reality, organizations often try out different structures. In fact, when an organization fails to meet its goals, blaming the failure on the current structure is not unusual. This is followed by trying a new organization model, complete with changing boxes, changing titles, and adding or subtracting authority layers.

Geographic structure. Large organizations have offices in different places. For example, there could be north, south, west, and east regions. The organizational structure could follow a regional structure (see figure 3.2).

Team structure. Many organizations with divisional structures adopt a team-based approach which is different from the organizational structures described above because *structure* is not permanent. When a new project or intervention is created, a team is formed to achieve the outcomes. Teams often have to deal with internal conflict issues, and difficulties can arise when team members belong to other unrelated teams at the same time. Teams may be formed by people from different departments. Teams tend to be self-directed working groups organized around work processes, with very flat spans of control and little formalization.

Matrix structure. This combines functional and product structures and aims to achieve the best of both worlds and to produce an efficient organizational structure. This is the most complex organizational structure. It is

Figure 3.2 Geographic Structure Example

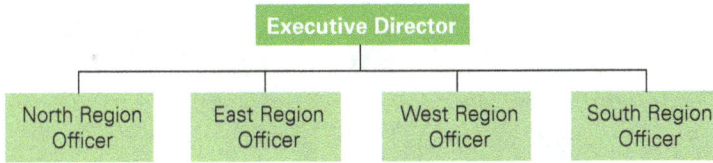

important to find a structure that works best for the organization because the wrong setup could hamper proper functioning in the organization. A matrix "has two axes, rather than a pyramid shape. The vertical hierarchy is overlaid by some lateral authority, influence or communication, and there are dual lines of responsibility, authority and accountability that violate the traditional 'one-boss,' principle or management" (Manage 2008 12, see figure 3.3).

Hybrid structure. An organization can also have a hybrid structure where more than one type of organizational structure is used.

Formal organizations are important because they provide accountability for work programs. They also clarify roles and responsibilities for people attached to the organization. Formal organizations help interpret institutional rules into the guidelines or protocols that define the services or goods for which the organization is responsible.

What role do informal networks play?

Think for a minute about your own organization. How does the work actually get done? Is information communicated through a formal chain of command? Is another system at work—one that relies on relationships outside the boxes and that is based solely on networks of individuals who share mutual trust, respect, and easy communication? The latter kind of system is referred to by management practitioners as an *informal organization*. Instead of following an organization chart, informal organizations work through systems of networks that bring individuals together to support the formal organization to get work done. Thus, the terms "informal organization" and "informal networks" are used interchangeably in this book.

This concept is not new. The social psychologist Jacob Moreno is credited with drawing the first "sociograms," or diagrams of interactions, of the rela-

Figure 3.3 **Matrix Structure Example**

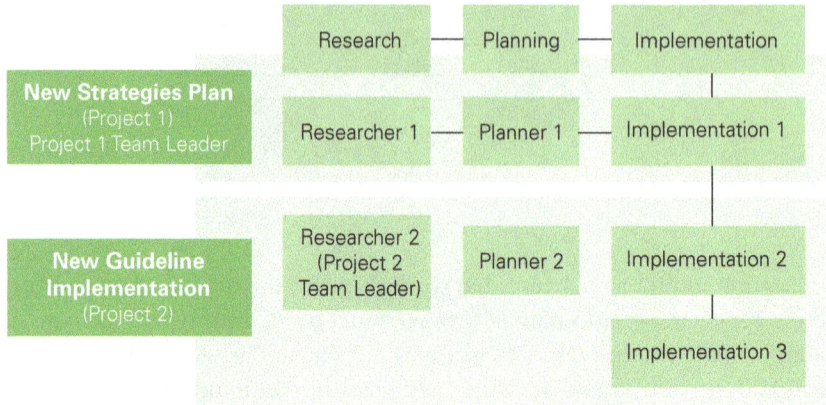

Figure 3.3 **Matrix Structure Example**

tionships of more than 2,000 students in New York State in 1934. Manfred Ketz De Vries (2001) summarized the situation well in his seminal publication *The Leadership Mystique.* He noted that even within organizations, the real power and authority are defined not only by the tangible (visible, documented, rational) policies, rules, regulations, and organizational charts, but by the intangible (hidden, undocumented, irrational) undercurrents of organizational culture and power dynamics among individuals in the organization. Figure 3.4 illustrates this notion, as well as the uncomfortable reality that most factors that make organizations work are hidden beneath the surface of what a manager typically manages.

More recently Malcolm Gladwell, in *The Tipping Point* (2000), helped speed the idea that social networks influence the uptake of ideas and trends in society. Today's successful managers and executives take note when employees use networks to get work done outside the formal organization structure and encourage that use.

What are the positive and negative aspects of informal networks?

Studies have shown that when a manager lacks awareness of the strength of informal networks in work settings, it significantly decreases performance and has a strong negative effect on the achievement of the organization's formal goals (Hollingsworth 1974). Besides their ability to streamline and speed up work within the formal organizational structure, informal networks can serve as an early warning system and, in general, as a way of gathering useful information. As Christian Waldstrøm found in a survey of the literature on informal networks, "This can take the form of identifying problems in the organization before they grow out of hand or spotting opportunities that would otherwise be missed" (2001, 31).

However, informal networks can be sources of problems as well, resulting from the creation of false rumors and conflicting loyalties within the organization and, perhaps especially, from a tendency to lead to counterproductive group thinking. "A group of individuals can easily develop their own set of norms ... which can develop into a[n] us/them situation toward other groups," Waldstrøm reported. "Specifically in situations where cooperation is required between the two groups, group thinking can have an adverse effect on both productivity and overall organizational morale" (2001, 31).

If information networks are ignored or misunderstood, they can throw up barriers to getting work done—barriers that are essentially invisible to the formal organization until they cause problems for the program. The mindful manager is aware that informal networks exist and tries to understand the key players within them. The manager uses them to further program goals or intervenes to prevent them from imposing obstacles. He or she may even want to reinforce or strengthen informal relationships to ensure an effective response to a crisis within the organization.

Figure 3.4 Visible and Hidden Organizational Processes

What's visible
Vision   Goals
Mission   Strategies
Structure   Operating policies
Job descriptions

Formal organization:
Rational forces

What's hidden   Power and influence patterns
                         Group dynamics
Informal organization: Conformity forces
Irrational forces   Impulsiveness
                         Feelings
                         Interpersonal; relations
                         Organizational culture
                         Individual needs

Source: Reproduced, with permission, from Ketz De Vries 2001; further permission required for reuse.

How do informal organizations support formal organizations to get the job done?

When programs fail and goals are not achieved, the first response often is to move organizational boxes around. To the question of what the new organization is intended to achieve, the answer might be "better collaboration," or "improved communication," or "new ways to get one part of the organization to work with other parts."

But how effective is this strategy? When we asked some of our own colleagues for their experience with organizational restructuring, many readily admitted that a lot of time and energy was spent to "get the boxes right" without much change in how people actually accomplished their work. At the same time, they agreed that effective collaboration was a key to delivering quality work on time and within budget.

The piece missing from the traditional management response is the recognition of the importance of informal networks. Dig deeply enough and you will find that informal collaborative networks, made up of like-minded individuals who work together to solve problems, support the work of most organizations. In those networks are people who both trust one another and enjoy working together. The networks succeed because they exist outside the organization chart and are not subject to typical carrot-and-stick incentives to behave within the boundaries of the formal structure.

We all know that within and outside formal organizations, individuals prefer to work with some people rather than others. How can those preferences be harnessed to support program implementation? In a 1993 *Harvard Business Review* article, David Krackhardt, of Carnegie Mellon University, and Jeff Hanson, the founder of Hanson Advisors in New York City, examined the question of how mapping employees' relationships can help managers harness the real power of organizations. Two decades later, that article is widely cited as having first shown managers, executives, and industry leaders the role that informal networks play in improving the way work gets done in organizations.

Krackhardt and Hanson argued that analyzing networks showed that the informal organization actually holds much of the power to achieve organizational goals. They wrote that by harnessing that power, the formal or authoritative organization can increase its ability to develop new ideas, support innovation, and improve how work is being delivered. According to Krackhardt and Hanson, the improvement happens through three networks: an advice network, a trust network, and a communications network. The three networks do not replace formal organizational structures but support them.

Advice networks. To solve an urgent problem, bounce an idea off a colleague, or get help in answering a difficult technical question, advice networks have been shown to be valuable. Advice networks are collections of respected individuals believed within the organization to be knowledgeable. These networks are important in most organizational settings but are considered indispensable in scientific and technology-based ones.

Trust networks. Individuals in organizations repeatedly use trust networks to share and discuss issues of a confidential nature, such as seeking personal employment advice or sharing office gossip, and for a host of other reasons. The formal authoritative organization is not typically the place for people to share this kind of information, and often the trust networks are smaller because individuals trust a smaller set of people within their network. These networks form for many reasons. Sometimes they rest on cultural similarities, on issues affecting a particular gender, and so on. These networks are useful in moving work forward. A common example is instances when assignments need to be staffed quickly. Through our trust networks we might seek names of possible candidates who will both be suitable for new work and fit into the work environment.

Communications networks. Communications networks allow important relationships to form among people who work on similar projects or who have offices near one another. For example, women sometimes prefer to have lunch with other women they work with, and men who share a passion for a sports team may want to talk to each other frequently about the score from last weekend's game. Communications networks are important to strengthen the way teams work together to get things done (see figure 3.5).

Use informal networking to enhance development projects

In the past decade, informal networking has changed from seeking out individuals inside an organization or in the immediate environment, to having access literally to the entire world. Computers, smartphones, and tools such as Skype have put people in touch with each other rapidly. The Internet has opened communications between the world's experts and everyday people using LISTSERV™ communities, interactive websites on specific topics, and, of course, Facebook, Twitter, and many professional networks. It is truly an urban myth that developing countries lack access to those networks be-

Figure 3.5 **A Typical Informal Network**

cause of limited Internet connectivity or that they cannot network because of language differences. In fact, the fastest growing group of online users is in the developing world. In many countries, phone use is almost exclusively cell phone use. Pay-as-you-go smartphones allow instant virtual networking and access to information from anywhere.

So what does this mean? Does having access to global knowledge help developing countries solve entrenched problems or help countries get work delivered to achieve results? A recent white paper for the Cisco Internet Business Solutions Group (Gill and Grant 2011) examined the problem of underresourcing of maternity services in developing countries. The study found that overall health care in many countries focused on acute care and needed to rethink how maternity services are delivered. A series of focus group workshops were held in Australia to determine how social networking, collaboration, and other information and communications technology solutions could improve the reach and quality of prenatal and postnatal care. Workshop findings suggested that implementing virtual, online maternity services that are based on collaboration and social networking technologies could dramatically lower costs and could improve prenatal and postnatal outcomes.

In 2010, a research study conducted by the World Bank evaluated the effect of female social networks for subsistence farmers in rural Uganda on a reemerging cash crop. This work was part of a larger, randomized controlled trial by the Bank titled "Gender Dimensions of Cotton Productivity in Uganda" (Baffes et al. 2010). The study was the first to show conclusively that the use of social networks has a causal effect on achieving agricultural outcomes. The study also concluded that using those networks can substitute for the traditional training programs that are widely used in developing countries and would allow communication of information at a much lower cost.

Analyze informal organizations to tap into their power

The best way to determine whether a person is a member of a particular informal network is to ask the person directly. Because one organization can have hundreds of informal networks, the best approach is charting the networks that are available around a topic of particular interest to the organization or a particular issue in which maximum collaboration, communication, and all-hands-on-deck support are needed. In addition, under-

---

BOX 3.1
Social Networks Help Get Work Done!

In the 1980s, an anthropologist at Xerox's Palo Alto Research Center made an interesting observation. Managers were trying to boost the productivity of the field service staff members, so instead of simply accepting their descriptions of work activities, the anthropologist actually followed field staff members around. He discovered that representatives ("reps") often made a point of spending time not with customers but with one another. They would gather in common areas, such as the parts warehouse or around the coffee machine, and would swap stories from the field.

Now imagine how a management consultant might view this observation— juicy pickings for recommending that the reps spend more time on the job or with the customer. But the consultant would miss the point. The anthropologist saw the social activities as an extremely valuable part of the day; the reps were acting as a community of professionals while providing one another with valuable insights into improving their work and learning how to solve customer problems more effectively.

Source: Brown and Gray 1995.

standing trust networks for key individuals who are expected to accomplish a great deal of work in a short time would be helpful. If key individuals' informal trust networks—the people on whom they depend informally—are known, then the formal structure can be broadened to include some of those people.

In *The Hidden Power of Social Networks*, Rob Cross and Andrew Parker (2004) outlined a simple technique for capturing network information that can show the myriad relationships involved in an issue or a program. Those maps can show how the informal organization helps work get done. Through the mapping process, pivotal individuals within the informal advisory, trust, and communications networks—as cited by Krackhardt and Hanson (1993)—can be identified and asked to support important new or ongoing work. The key individuals are not always those who are the highest placed within the formal organizations, as can be seen in the following example of an advisory network.

In the simple formal organization shown in figure 3.6, Henry is the most powerful person; Nigel and Regina are in a direct reporting line to him. Julia, George, Anne, and Andrés function in a subordinate role within this organization. This formal organization chart (figure 3.7) clearly outlines the flow of formal communication.

However, in the informal advisory network shown in figure 3.7, George is the most influential person. Each member of the team calls on George for advice most of the time. Only Julia asks Regina for advice, and she depends on both George and Ruth to help her get her job done (Ruth is outside the formal organization).

In the informal trust network (see figure 3.8), we find an altogether different set of interactions at play. The most trusted individual in the network is Regina, but Julia has the trust of nearly all other individuals as well. Anne is outside the trust network completely, a fact of considerable interest when analyzing networks. This network is used at times of organizational turbulence, or when fear is high. People tend to use a particular group of trusted individuals with whom they believe they can share important professional information and from whom they get advice that is "off the record."

An informal communications network is also at work. This network is often a more closed network of people who work together on a daily basis, sit near each other, and communicate regularly about a project or the office comings and goings. These individuals work on the same team or share work deadlines, yet they may or may not like each other very much. Sometimes one person seems to be "in the know" about office politics. This network is important to understand as well (see box 3.2).

Including informal networks does not ensure that a project will be successful. But not understanding how those networks work and failing to manage the project environment to make use of them will jeopardize any chance for success.

Figure 3.6 Formal Organization Chart

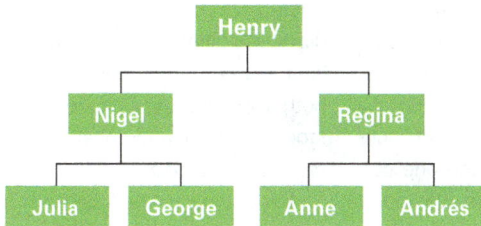

Figure 3.7 Informal Advisory Network

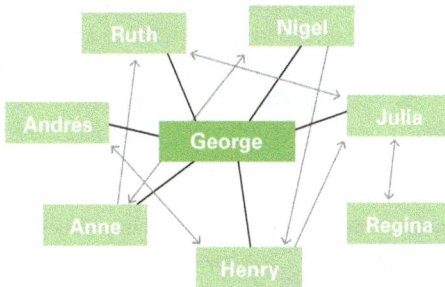

Figure 3.8 Informal Trust Network

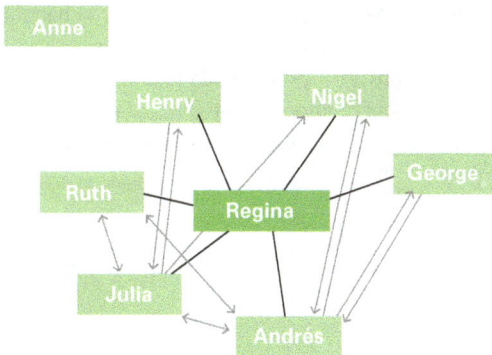

BOX 3.2

Informal Networks: Facilitators or Saboteurs?

In a small, ethnically diverse country in the Southern Hemisphere, where "everyone knows everyone," a regional development bank was asked to help the government pilot a project to introduce a modern health insurance scheme that would benefit the lowest income quintile of the population. This new scheme was already working in a number of countries in the region, and the country assumed that it would replace the one currently operating. The current system worked in some places, but coverage was low, as was citizen satisfaction with the model. The regional development bank began to establish a formal working structure for the new project team, which included both national and international staff.

Support for the project was gaining momentum across established groups, such as local leaders and important civil society groups. The project worked hard to keep powerful stakeholders in the loop. However, one shortcoming on the part of the development bank was its failure to recognize the informal relationships forming within the project team. Project managers were stressing the importance of following rules and norms established by the new organization and also stressed that the team work closely within the formal structure during the project planning and initial implementation stages. This meant that old channels of communication were cut off from providing input and were more or less kept out of the loop.

As the project advanced, members of the new formal team were again discouraged from talking about the project to anyone outside the project team, thus shutting down possible communication with once-important networks of trusted country experts. This ended up jeopardizing the ultimate success of the project, as we later learned. The real power structure, once both apparent and opaque, was neither understood nor given appropriate consideration as the project proceeded.

For example, two local staff members hired by the regional bank's project team were members of a different religious group than most of the other staff. Unfortunately, that group was stigmatized and distrusted in the project environment. By the time the project team understood the extent to which important informal networks were being ignored, damage was already done to the project in terms of reputation and attitudes. "If we had managed the informal network better, we could have neutralized or even avoided much of the negative criticism, most of which was unfounded."

The pilot project was ultimately successful in implementing a health insurance scheme for the lowest quintile of the population. However, the project was never adopted by the government. The health insurance scheme was not implemented nationally to benefit the most underprivileged population.

The lesson learned is that both formal and informal networks are critical to the success of development projects and programs.

Source: Rosalia Rodriquez Garcia, World Bank.

Use informal networks in times of organizational crisis

Informal networks can be crucial in avoiding failure in times of organizational crisis. Organizational theorists have defined "crisis" in various ways, but for our purposes, Krackhardt and Stern offer a workable definition by defining a crisis as "a situation facing an organization which requires that the organization, under time constraints, engage in new, untested, unlearned behaviors in order to obtain or maintain its desired goal states" (1988, 125). In this formulation, a crisis may have external sources, or it may result from events within an organization or project.

In their research, Krackhardt and Stern (1988) demonstrated that the nature of the informal networks within an organization can either help it respond to a crisis or exacerbate the crisis by interfering with cooperation among program participants. They warn that organizations in which management ignores or does not cultivate informal communications can produce dysfunctional networks by concentrating friendships within organizational subunits. If one thinks about the relationships described earlier, that means that information is confined within specific parts of the formal organization rather than flowing across the organization. As a result, vital communications are also constrained, and in times of crisis, such constraint can become a fundamental and perhaps fatal flaw.

Ask these key questions when using Rule 3

- Have you identified the informal networks within your organization?
- Do you have a sense of how they operate and who is involved?
- Are the networks useful or dysfunctional in accomplishing your organization's goals?
- How can you use them to your strategic advantage—as sources of information, as informal communications networks, or as vehicles for streamlining and speeding up work?
- How would they help or hurt if the organization faced a crisis?

References

Baffes, John, Madhur Guatam, Kenneth L. Leonard, Laoura Maratou, and Sarah Ssewanyana. 2010. "The Gender Dimension of Cotton Productivity in Uganda." Gender Action Plan proposal, World Bank, Washington, DC.

Brown, John Seely, and Estee Solomon Gray. 1995. "The People Are the Company." *Fast Company*, November. http://www.fastcompany.com/26238/people-are-company.

Cross, Rob, and Andrew Parker. 2004. *The Hidden Power of Social Networks*. Boston: Hanologies Can Improve Prenatal and Postnatal Outcomes, and Lower Costs." White Paper, Cisco Internet Business Solutions Group.

Gladwell, Malcolm. 2000. *The Tipping Point: How Little Things Can Make a Big Difference*. Boston: Little, Brown and Company.

Görgens, Marelize, and Jody Zall Kusek. 2009. *Making Monitoring and Evaluation Systems Work: A Capacity Development Tool Kit*. Washington, DC: World Bank.

Hollingsworth, A. T. 1974. "Perceptual Accuracy of the Informal Organization as a Determinant of the Effectiveness of Formal Leaders." *Journal of Economics and Business* 27 (1): 75–78.

Ketz De Vries, Manfred. 2001. *The Leadership Mystique: Leading Behavior in the Human Enterprise*. London: FT Press.

Krackhardt, David, and Jeff Hanson. 1993. "Informal Networks: The Company behind the Chart." *Harvard Business Review* 71 (4): 104–11.

Krackhardt, David, and Robert N. Stern. 1988. "Informal Networks and Organizational Crisis: An Experimental Simulation." *Social Psychology Quarterly* 51 (2): 123–40.

Moreno, Jacob L. 1934. *Who Shall Survive? A New Approach to the Problem of Human Interrelations*. Washington, DC: Nervous and Mental Disease Publishing Co.

Waldstrøm, Christian. 2001. "Informal Networks in Organizations: A Literature Review." DDL (Det Danske Ledelsesbarometer) Working Paper No. 2, Aarhus School of Business, Aarhus University, Denmark.

Unclog the pipes

A bad system will defeat a good person every time.

—W. Edwards Deming

Imagine that you direct a new and innovative program that your government has created to pay poor people to move into government-built housing. Recent evaluation data from the London School of Economics have shown that living in one's own home helps people begin to move out of poverty. This finding represents a major change from the current practice of giving poor people monthly disbursements to spend for housing in any way they choose. You are about to launch a major project in three districts that will move 1,600 poor people, who are living either with relatives or on the street, into homes of their own. The United Nations (UN) is the primary funder of this program and created a fast-track instrument to channel new funds to ongoing programs in less than one month.

One day you get an e-mail offering new, emergency funding to move 500 additional people into homes by the end of the year. While this offer is tempting, it will also mean significant increases in work for your small team. Your response is a tentative yes, but you need to revise your project plan and make certain that you can get the required approvals from the technical and legal staff to carry out the expanded undertaking.

After a number of inquiries with your team and legal staff, you are assured that taking on this new work is possible and that deadlines could be met. The UN representative says that she needs only a few days to complete the transactions on her end, once she receives a funding request. After that, a simple transfer of funds should occur. These funds are available for only 30 days, so you begin the process immediately. Your group is requested to begin working immediately on the assignment, with the assumption that the new funding agreements will be completed. As project director, you mobilize your teams, shift work, and begin the new assignment.

Unfortunately, five weeks pass and you still have not received the promised funds. After calling the UN adviser who requested the new work, you communicate that you will need to stop work on the new assignment because you have run out of funds. She is shocked. She thought the transfer of funds was accomplished weeks ago. Finally, upon inquiry with the budget department, she finds out that somehow your request was never received, nor was it followed up on by the group who would make the transfer. Now the UN money is no longer available. Your adviser profusely apologizes and promises to look for other funding sources. But this will take time. Sound familiar?

Blocked work processes can slow or stop work

In most organizations, work is done through a series of activity steps called a "process." In what is often referred to as a "business process," work activities function together to accomplish a specific organizational goal. "Process management" means applying a systematic approach to making an organization's processes—its work flow—more effective, more efficient, and more capable of adapting to an ever-changing environment. The goal of process management is to reduce human error and miscommunication and to focus the process participants on the requirements of their roles. Unfortunately, blocked processes can literally cause a project, or part of it, to fail. Defining the steps in a work process, or knowing how it functions, is the first step in being able to manage it to avoid bottlenecks or even failure.

The term "bottleneck" originally referred to constriction in traffic flow but now describes

> a point of congestion in any system from computer networks to a factory assembly line. In such a system, there is always some process, task, machine, etc., that is the limiting factor preventing a greater throughput and thus determines the capacity of the entire system. Knowing the bottleneck allows increasing the flow by improving just one process in the system rather than all its remain-

ing parts. Vice versa, if there is a bottleneck, nothing done elsewhere in the value stream can improve the throughput. (Leporis and Kralova 2010, 1; quoting Goldratt and Cox 1984)

The focus on the role of business processes in organizational success began in the 1980s with the introduction of "total quality management," followed by "process reengineering" a decade later. The main point in the process movement is that process effectiveness and efficiency are at the heart of an organization's performance. A central premise is that if the work process—the steps taken to deliver an end product or service—is flawed, performance will be degraded, and no amount of work will compensate for the poor performance caused by a flawed work process (Endeavor Management 2010). Numerous excellent books, courses, and other literature have been written over the last two decades on how to remove bottlenecks in work processes. In this guide, we offer suggestions on how to recognize potential bottlenecks in work processes that can cause projects to fail and how to "manage them out of your project."

What is a process?

Everything an organization does is a function of internal and external processes, whether we recognize that fact or not. A "process" is the set of activities that accomplishes some business function. In her book on process mapping, Sue Conger (2011) says that in a perfect model, a process consists of the following components:

- Input—the information that is used in the process
- Process steps—ways that transform or otherwise manipulate the input
- Output—a good or service that results from the process
- Feedback—the information that takes the form of monitoring and metrics on output quality and that is used to regulate and improve the process.

We care about processes because you cannot manage what you do not know or understand. Processes help define both simple and complicated functions. A *simplified process,* for example, is defining the steps it would take in the example described earlier, in which a request is made to increase a work scope and in return increase the budget to fund the additional work. A *complicated process* might be the regulatory process to approve a new vaccine.

Still, even for a simple process, more than one organization can be involved. In the case above, funding a relatively simple task order involved two agencies: a government organization and the funder, a UN organization. To look at the entirety of this process, it is necessary to understand the flow of work within and across the two organizations. The UN required a funding request to start the process. However, to do so, the government needed to follow certain rules within its own organization to be able to deliver the request. Bottlenecks can occur within the process of one or both organizations.

In business processes, two main types of bottlenecks occur—short term and long term. *Short-term bottlenecks* results from temporary problems. A good example is the case when a key team member is temporarily reassigned to another project, thereby removing a critical part of the project's work flow. If no one else is qualified to fill the gap, backlogs could occur until the missing team member returns.

Long-term bottlenecks are no less frequent than the short-term variety, and they create the greatest frustrations for managers and the greatest risk to a project. An example is a process in a project that requires the approval of one government official who is notoriously slow in processing paperwork. Or a long-term bottleneck could be the result of the absence of a step that is needed to ensure a workflow through the process.

Identifying bottlenecks and fixing them are necessary to prevent work processes from simply stopping working, with the resulting lost revenue, dissatisfied customers, wasted time, poor quality products or services, and high stress on team members.

To learn how to analyze bottlenecks, take as an example the simple process of getting new funding from the UN. The process might look like the flow diagram in figure 4.1.

Find and eliminate bottlenecks

A simple way to understand whether bottlenecks are affecting your project is to use flowcharts. Flowcharts are generally known as "process maps," and they can be invaluable in identifying where bottlenecks are occurring. It is not realistic to map out every process for every program or project. A large project may comprise hundreds of processes. However, most managers have a pretty good idea what part of the project is the most costly, or seems to be driving up overall costs. This is a good place to start. Go for the 80–20 rule: Identify the 20 percent of the processes that account for 80 percent of all project costs. That is where eliminating bottlenecks is likely to make the biggest difference in getting the work done on time and within budget.

Figure 4.1 **Funding Flow Diagram**

Funder Request

```
Funder Request
     │
     ▼
Team prepares  →  Legal     →  Technical
request           approves      approves
     │
     ▼
Approved
request
     │
     └──────→  Request sent  →  Sent to      Accounts
               to U.N.          budget review  review
                                      │
                                      ▼
                                Funds transfer
                                to government
                                program
```

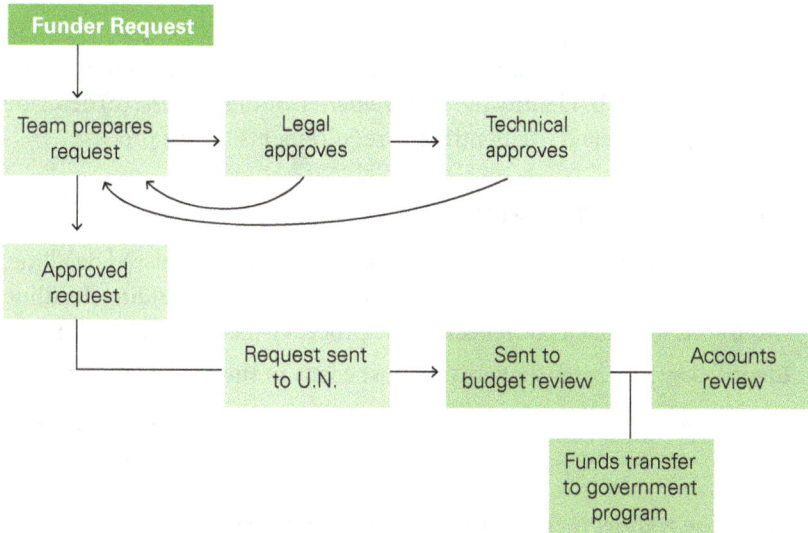

Other signs that a work process is not allowing work to freely flow through it are:

- *Long wait times.* For example, work is delayed because you are waiting for a product, a report, or more information. Perhaps materials spend time waiting between steps of a business or manufacturing process.
- *Backlogged work.* Too much work piles up at one end and not enough at the other end.
- *Missed deadlines or falling behind schedule.* Clients are dissatisfied because work is regularly not received on time, or when promised, or, as in the case described above, you are missing out on opportunities because of missed deadlines.
- *Tension.* High tension levels are noticeable within the project or organization.
- *Business processes develop and change over time.* Often these processes evolve to meet new business needs. Over time, changes to business processes, and changes to the environment that these processes operate within, can cause them to become inefficient. Analysis of business processes can identify inefficiencies, and their correction can reduce costs and improve the quality of their outputs.

A Simple Method to Review a Work Process
(adapted from netmba.com)

Four important activities underpin a process review: (a) determine which process to analyze; (b) identify the requirements for the process; (c) describe the current process; and (d) identify the requirements for the process.

Determine which business processes to analyze

- Look for signs of a bottleneck, such as long wait times, a missed deadline, or large work backlogs. (In the case above, missing the funding deadline was a sure sign that a bottleneck in the process existed somewhere.)
- Identify key processes that are the most costly in the organization.
- Use the 80–20 rule: 20 percent of processes = 80 percent of project costs.

Identify the requirements for the business process

- Interview key process participants.
- Ask what they do and why they do it.
- Ascertain what information and other inputs are needed to perform each task. Identify the source for each input.
- Identify the outputs (or deliverable parts) of each task, who the recipients are, and why they need what they receive.
- Conduct group interviews and brainstorming sessions.
- Use group sessions to validate and refine the information you have received once you've gathered initial information about a process through one-on-one interviews. This is an excellent way to clear up misconceptions of individuals within the process.
- Summarize the information you have received and distribute it to the process participants. This should include both participants you have interviewed and others that you did not interview.

Document the current business process

- Create a process flowchart (also known as a process map).
- Flowcharts may be prepared manually or with the use of a chart creation program. Word processors and spreadsheet programs with charting functionality may be used. Programs designed specifically for the purpose of drawing flowcharts are particularly well suited to the task.

Identify the requirements for the process

- Evaluate the activities performed in each task: Are the activities efficient? Are they all focused on meeting the task objective?
- Compare the results from individual interviews. Look for inconsistencies. For instance, does one step in the process deliver something to the next step that is not used in the next step?
- Identify activities and task outputs that are unnecessary.
- Sketch the business process from scratch based on the business process requirements identified during interviews and brainstorming sessions. Compare this process flow with the flowchart of the existing process.
- Look for potential bottlenecks that can be managed out of the process.

Once you find a problem in the work process, or a bottleneck, take action. Whether the problem is wait times or the flow of supplies, ask yourself whether the bottleneck is the result of a staffing issue. If it is, correct it. You may need to increase your staff levels only at peak times in the project. If it is a procedural issue, find out where the breakdown in policy is occurring. If it is a personnel issue, make a change. As the project manager, you must recognize that the potential for a bottleneck is always present. It is important for you to be vigilant and to train your staff to recognize the signs of possible bottlenecks. In the case described in box 4.1, a simple process review uncovered a bottleneck that if identified earlier would have resulted in a significant improvement in the performance of one organization in the government of the U.S. state of Texas. The moral of the story is: It is important to look for bottlenecks. You will likely find them.

In the case of getting the UN funding, a process review showed that there was too much red tape in the government organization to possibly meet the deadline set by the UN adviser. Simply adding new funds to an existing funding source probably did not need to involve the legal staff, or even the technical experts for that matter, since the money was to increase ongoing work. If those reviews had been eliminated, the deadline would have been met.

Assign process managers to move work along

Not all processes are as simple as the one presented above. In fact, many business processes have hundreds of steps. Where processes are complex, mapping the work flow may seem like an enormous task, but the process map offers a way of subdividing a complex process into discrete and manageable pieces, thereby making the task of eliminating bottlenecks considerably easier.

BOX 4.1
Find Out What's Taking So Long

The comptroller's office of the U.S. state of Texas developed an interesting approach to process management that could be done with the resources at hand, without involving outside experts or spending funds on detailed studies. The office developed an internal review process called the Renaissance Project that was designed to involve people from across the agency to take a fresh look at internal management issues.

Employee volunteers, who worked on it during only part of their workday for a few weeks, carried out the project and made recommendations that were presented to a management committee and to affected agencies for reaction, feedback, and usually implementation. These endeavors were not large process reengineering projects. They normally addressed routine processes, such as correspondence, that the agency believed people who were close to the work or affected by it could improve. Generally they were successful in doing so.

One issue examined was approval of rules. The agency continually issues rules and policy guidance on tax questions. The rules are developed by a policy group and approved by the central Tax Policy Committee, a committee of upper-level policy people and central management. Final approval of the rules requires a long series of sign-offs by affected divisions—Tax Policy, Audit, Enforcement, Revenue Administration, Revenue Processing, Accounts Management, Legal, Open Records, and so on. Taxpayers had complained that the release of new rules, which generally were previewed to taxpayers in draft form for comment, was taking too long. A Renaissance team was formed to look at the process.

Basically, the team tracked a sample of rules through the process. How long did it take, on average, to complete each step of the process? This examination was very simple. It is just that no one had ever bothered to do it before.

The Renaissance team found that one person was the bottleneck responsible for about 85 percent of all delays. He simply waited until he had a light workday to review all the rules at once, which meant that some sat on his desk for a week or more. The team recommended requiring that rules be acted on—positively, negatively, or otherwise—within two business days of being logged into a division and that a person in Tax Policy be in charge of tracking the rule packages (the file with the rules and associated documentation) at all times. That change was made, and about three weeks were squeezed out of the review process, because not only was time in the Legal Department reduced, but other divisions became more aware of the need to move the packages.

Eventually the process was automated in electronic form, which greatly improved the office's ability to track timing, status, and current location of documents. It also allowed simultaneous reviews where that made sense. In other words, Audit and Enforcement could review and comment on the rule change at the same time. This change saved further time for the system.

The moral of the story is that simple answers to problems are often available if someone will just take the time to look for them—and if management is willing to change a process to make improvements.

Source: Comptroller's office, state of Texas.

Process managers help work to get done

In the nomenclature of process management, process managers are the "executors" of the process (ITSM MD 2011). Those executors are special teams or individuals who ensure that the "work" is being moved through the steps in the order described by the approved process. They are responsible for managing the inputs and outputs of each step, and they ensure that the final outcome desired is achieved.

Typically the individuals who make good process managers are "people" persons. They need to be able to cajole others into achieving their work tasks as promised, on time, and with quality. Reworking or sending work back through the process to be revised adds to the time it takes to get the work accomplished.

But good people skills are not the end of a good process manager's tool kit. Possibly even more important is that good process managers must be comfortable with sifting through details to identify problems that may have occurred in each process step and figuring out how to get the work back on track. The two characteristics of a process manager are sometimes at odds with each other. Thus, having a person who is good at focusing on details and who can work well with other team members—and with external actors—makes for an effective process management team.

Time is the enemy

Delays in projects can be their death. Donors can become frustrated, the client government can become frustrated, and your organization's management can become frustrated. In development, some delays probably are inevitable, but in many cases, the problem is simply a failure to focus on the internal processes that are inherent in the project. Failure happens when (a) no clear sense exists of what the processes are; (b) processes are not broken into discrete steps; and (c) the time involved in each step of the process is not measured. A step-by-step examination can yield big dividends and avoid project failure from the sheer inertia that can overwhelm any unwatched process sequence.

- Do you understand the processes involved in each of your project's key activities?
- Identify which ones are contributing to higher costs, or likely problems in program performance.
- Do you know the business requirements for that process, and does the current process support these requirements?
- If bottlenecks are identified in the current process, have you and your team met with key stakeholders to identify ways to manage out these bottlenecks?
- Have you considered making someone in the project responsible for process management—for making sure that bottlenecks are identified and eliminated and that the process is monitored for the development of future bottlenecks?
- What possible bottlenecks are simply not fixable, and are there other solutions to the problem?

References

Conger, Sue. 2011. *Process Mapping and Management*. New York: Business Expert Press.

Endeavor Management's Knowledge Center. 2010. "Defining Process Owner, Process Leader, and/or Process Manager." Posted April 29, 2010. http://change articles.wordpress.com/2010/04/29/defining-process-owner-process-leader-andor-process-manager/.

Goldratt, E. M., and J. Cox. 1984. *The Goal. Excellence in Manufacturing*. Croton-on-Hudson: North River Press.

ITSM MD (IT Services Management—From Maryland). 2011. "Process Owner versus Process Manager." Posted July 27, 2011. http://itsmmd.com/2011/07/27/process-owner-versus-process-manager.

Leporis, M., and Z. Kralova. 2010. "A Simulation Approach to Production Line Bottleneck Analysis." International Conference on Cybernetics and Informatics, Vyšńa Boca, Slovak Republic.

http://en.wikipedia.org/wiki/business_analysis

http://www.unescap.org/tid/publications/tipub2558_chapt2/pdf

http://www.netmba.com/operations/process/analysis

Build
the ship
as it sails

Make
it about
the how

Keep your
champions
close but
your critics
closer

Fail-Safe

Unclog
the pipes

Informal
networks
matter —
work with
them

RULE 5

Build the ship as it sails

Your best teacher is your last mistake.—Ralph Nader

Imagine this: You are the new minister of budgeting and finance in a country known for historically having a less-than-transparent governing policy, a growing and demanding population base fueled by access to mass media, a high dependency on foreign aid, and poor levels of service delivery. Recently, in parts of the country, citizens have demonstrated to demand that government improve basic services. Citizens are using social media at a level formerly unseen to share their displeasure with the government. Currently, no valid systems are in place to measure whether services are slow, costly, or of acceptable quality. You have heard citizen complaints about long lines to get into the post office every day at five o'clock, after work, and often people are told to come back the next day because of a prompt five-thirty closure. The same problem occurs at public health clinics, which are few and far between and often close at three in the afternoon. This is unfortunate because most working people need to use those services in the evening, after they have finished work. Improving service delivery was one of the promises made when the new government was elected.

During a recent international conference you learned that successful countries are using a number of strategies to improve the way services are being delivered to citizens. A number of ideas were presented, but three seem most replicable in your own country. They are (a) go for quick wins, to show citizens that you will provide immediate relief to real problems, while getting their buy-in for longer-term solutions; (b) keep implementation flexible, to test innovative or early designs to see what works and what does not. Flexible implementation allows for learning, feedback, and improvements before scaling up to larger service areas. (c) Be willing to make mistakes and correct them. Successful countries allow programs to make mistakes, learn from those mistakes, and improve how services are delivered. If mistakes are made and remedies are implemented, the government department is not penalized but given incentives to address the mistakes.

After the conference, you briefed the president and other ministers about what you learned and discussed how these principles could be used to improve services in the country. One minister acknowledged that many of the services in the country were being delivered by complicated programs with performance goals that would take years to achieve. However, there are other problems that could be addressed quickly. For example, in the area of local government, citizens were complaining that post offices were open in the middle of the day when most people worked. The post office happened to be the place where citizens went to get licenses for marriage, to certify births, and to apply for driver's licenses, and so it was a very important service center. Most people worked until five o'clock in the evening, and the post office closed promptly at five thirty, meaning that people had to take time off from work to do ordinary business.

Reform of the post office was part of a large program to improve local services across the country. Included in the program were building new local government facilities, possibly sharing services across the country, and reforming how elections were to take place. Several consultants worked on the programs, and complex reports were under way on various options and recommendations.

Although the government believed that focusing on longer-term goals was the right strategy to reform the country, the ordinary citizens wanted to see and feel improvements in their day-to-day lives—now!

The minister of communications offered to be the first to consider where postal services could be improved to find some "quick wins." The minister held a workshop with key stakeholders and identified a number of service improvements that could be implemented almost immediately and at low cost. These included longer hours of operation (opening earlier in the morning and staying open later), increased numbers of qualified staff members to address problems, and a commitment to process licenses in three days. Given the population's wide adoption of social media as a communications tool, a complaints line via Twitter was opened. Success stories were published, and the government defined four post office services that could be transacted online in the future.

Fourteen post offices were established as models where the new services could be tested to find what worked best and why. Post offices that failed to show improvement were given three chances to try again, as long as they could show that with each new effort, improvements were made to systems and services. At the end of nine months, the ministry would analyze what service changes were working best and why. The analyses would be incorporated into the final model that would be rolled out across the country.

Because of the "instant" reform measures that made a tangible difference in people's lives, and because of the transparency in setting and reporting on medium- to long-term objectives, the postal service won an award for being the best service provider in the country. This positive example made other ministries take notice and follow suit. Soon, two other ministries had started similar initiatives.

Quick wins are important

Leading implementation management experts, including Alex Laufer, Robert Schaffer, Ron Ashkenas, and John Kotter, have written about the catalytic effect of short-term wins. In the preceding story, immediate wins were critical to win over both champions and critics of the government. Improving the postal service, used by everyone, increased overall citizen satisfaction. In addition, those ministers willing to start similar efforts became new champions to help move the reform forward.

More than ever development practitioners are calling for a show of evidence about what works and why. In doing so, many are questioning the value of implementing projects to demonstrate short-term wins in favor of researching what works in the long term. In their book *Rapid Results,* Robert Schaffer and Ron Ashkenas wrote, tongue in cheek:

> Watch out, management is saying! We know that if you focus on short-term results this will necessitate moves that are essentially unhealthy. You could be advancing tactical gains at the expense of strategic gains. You could be wasting resources on the wrong efforts. You could be investing in the wrong products or services. (2005, viii)

The authors of this book were saying that these managers were missing out on the benefit of learning what works before investing in research, or building the ship as it sails.

Certainly development impact research has gotten more than its 15 minutes of fame. We look to these researchers for answers about where to invest in countries and where not to invest. However, spending the years necessary to learn what really works and why in one setting may not be suitable in another setting.

There is room both for a long-term understanding of what works and why, and for finding immediate solutions for known problems. Citizens want government to deliver better service today. They do not want to wait for answers from research that may be years away.

Be flexible during implementation

As Rule 1 reinforced, avoiding failure means paying attention to how work is getting done, and not only to what needs to be done and why. When a project involves many people working over an extended period, it is hard for the managers planning it to predict all the activities and work streams that will be needed. In a constantly changing development environment, the efficient management of project implementation is a key factor in avoiding project failure. Zubair Bhatti, leading a World Bank reform program in Punjab, Pakistan, reflected that "the only thing that matters is that things matter on the ground. While it's useful to have a plan, we must be prepared to change things on a daily basis to adapt to realities on the ground."

It doesn't matter how sound the policy or how well designed the project is. If an organization doesn't pay close attention to management details—how it will work on the ground—the result will be failure.

Throughout implementation, managers, staff members, and project stakeholders ought to be able to receive regular answers to the following questions:

- Is the project delivering goods and services on time and within budget?
- Is the project meeting the expectations of those it intends to serve at that moment in time?
- Do citizens (or consumers) have a reasonable expectation that if they report problems or complaints some action will be taken related to their concern?
- Are problems identified and fixed within a reasonable time?

Each of the questions might be answered with a simple yes or no, but that would provide little information on how well the project is being managed. If someone measured how often each question was answered yes or no, then a record of whether or not the service was meeting the expectations of its stakeholders would be created. In other words, measures are needed to help track if the project is or is not meeting its goals during implementation. These "results" measures should be tracked throughout the implementation of the program. Only through regular tracking and reporting on the selected measures or indicators, along with regular feedback about what is and what is not working, can an organization know whether a project is on track.

In 2007, Gujarat became the first state in India to introduce results reporting to improve the delivery of care in major government health facilities (State of Gujarat 2011). After it introduced performance results reporting, the state began to see important improvements in how health facilities were being managed. The effort began after identification of numerous problems that included limited capacity, lack of standards and guidelines, poor sanitation and cleanliness in hospitals, staff shortages in every category, buildings in damaged and poor condition, absence of patient satisfaction monitoring, and a systematic lack of measures for patient safety.

In Gujarat, the state began by identifying problems in the delivery of its health service. Managers then developed a set of results indicators that could be tracked to identify where improvements were being made or where problems continued to exist in various parts of the delivery systems. This allowed the state to better manage the delivery of services and stay on the track of problems. Five years after this program began, the state of Gujarat had become a model across India. Even with numerous improvements, leadership has vowed to continue to search out delivery problems and fix them.

In figure 5.1, we present a simple model that describes what it means to implement, learn, and improve. The logic behind this model is that all new projects should be tested on a small scale to see what works and what does not, to learn from that, and to continue to improve the project before scaling it up to a larger service area. A project can, of course, be rolled out at once in small service areas, but in large areas, such as in the example of Gujarat, it is sensible,

Figure 5.1 **Feedback-Learning Loop**

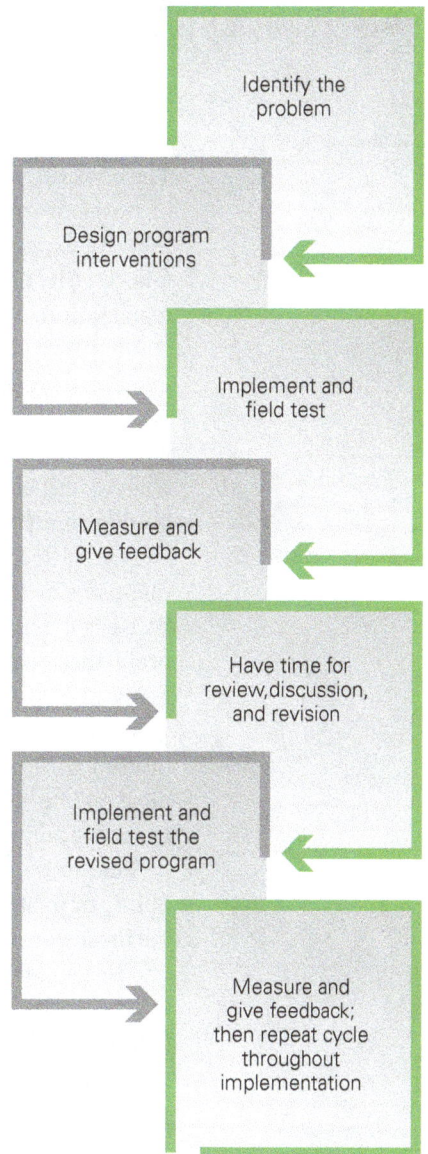

Identify the problem

Design program interventions

Implement and field test

Measure and give feedback

Have time for review, discussion, and revision

Implement and field test the revised program

Measure and give feedback; then repeat cycle throughout implementation first, to test the concepts only in key parts of the service delivery chain, where performance can be tracked and monitored.

Be willing to make mistakes and correct them

The book titled *Better by Mistake* (2011), by Alina Tugend, presents a number of stories from different industries, both public and private. Tugend shows that the expectation of perfection has directly contributed to catastrophic failures. She points out that mistakes should be thought of as something to manage and learn from.

In 2011, when we were developing research for this book, we spoke with many colleagues from different international development organizations. We sought out professionals who were working on projects that we knew were having problems. We sought lessons about what happened after the team identified problems and how they chose to correct them. In more than 20 different problem projects, we could not find a single project manager who admitted that mistakes were somehow made along the way—not by them, not by the client, not by the situation, not by anything. We were told that circumstances beyond anyone's control created the opportunity for problems to occur, and they did. We found that response curious and looked further.

We found that some projects were abruptly canceled, and others were infused with new capital, when they did not go as expected. We found almost no one who would utter the word "failure," and many who told us that changing political circumstances lay behind the problems.

That those working in international organizations are reluctant to admit failure or mistakes raises many questions to think and write about. Addressing those questions is beyond the scope of this book, however. Perhaps someone else will wish to write about the phenomenon.

The Avahan story, presented in box 5.1, describes how one organization admitted a major failure in the design of one of its programs and faced a choice: go back to the drawing board or give up. As you will read, the organization chose the former and ended up with a winning program.

In a completely different setting, the recent presidential election in the United States offered an example of the dangers of introducing a new program without "testing and learning."

BOX 5.1

Learning from Program Failure—Building the Ship as It Sails

Long-distance truckers in India are particularly vulnerable to acquiring HIV and other sexually transmitted infections. A number of programs existed to offer health services, but few people were taking advantage of them. The Indian government asked Avahan, a program run by the Bill and Melinda Gates Foundation, to work with one of its partners, the foundation arm of India's largest trucking company, Transport Corporation of India Foundation, to design a program to improve health service uptake. An intervention was designed to establish 36 facilities along major highways to offer health and health education services and to track the incidence of new HIV and other sexually transmitted infections. The program included a strong emphasis on regularly monitoring and evaluating how each facility was performing. Within two years, program data indicated that despite a national presence, critical program gaps remained. A behavior tracking survey conducted in mid-2005 revealed that program awareness among the target population was only 12 percent and that service uptake was only 7 percent. Other data revealed that approximately 40 percent to 50 percent of services were inadvertently directed at individuals other than the highest-risk, long-distance truckers. In addition, uptake of services was low in large locations, where service points had low visibility.

The Avahan program managers were faced with a choice: Should they end the investment in this poorly performing program or design a different implementation strategy, with the aim of servicing fewer sites while reaching the greatest number of vulnerable truckers? Using the abundance of implementation data on what worked and what did not, the Avahan managers realized that a solution would be to halve the number of intervention areas to 17, but with increased service access points within a site intelligently placed to maximize coverage of long-distance truckers. Other changes created a trucker-friendly, standardized interface that was staffed with trucker peers across all locations, to increase brand recall and credibility, and the (unchanged) budget was used to intensify services in the smaller number of locations. This strategy soon paid off: Outreach and clinic services uptake doubled, condom sales increased 50 percent, and 85 percent to 90 percent of services reached long-distance truckers.

Source: Kusek and Wilson 2009.

References

Calleam Consulting Ltd. 2012. "Project Orca: 2012 U.S. Presidential Campaign. Why Projects Fail." November 30. http://calleam.com/WTPF/?p=4146.

Kotter, John P. 1996. *Leading Change.* Cambridge: Harvard University Press.

Kusek, Jody, and David Wilson. 2009. "The Marriage of Business Principles and Public Health in India," Global HIV Program Evaluation Note, World Bank, Washington, DC.

BOX 5.2

The 2012 Presidential Campaign

Synopsis:

The 2012 U.S. presidential election illustrates how the failure to test a program properly can cause an embarrassing failure at a critical time. To help manage the logistics of their Election Day get-out-the-vote push, both the Obama and Romney campaigns developed "operational management" systems that would provide real-time tracking of voter turnout in the key battleground states. Providing critical insight into what was happening in the field, the systems fed data from volunteers at the polling stations back to campaign headquarters. Allowing the campaign to optimize the use of the available field workers, the systems provided the data needed to ensure that volunteers were directed to those precincts and counties where they were needed most.

With smartphone-enabled volunteers at each polling station, the systems channeled streams of real-time data back to campaign headquarters. By crunching the numbers, the systems gave their respective campaigns the "big picture" as the day progressed. With the systems up and running, the campaign had information and control. If the system failed, however, the volunteers were in the dark and would have to piece things together on the basis of hundreds of phone conversations.

According to available reports, the Obama system (called "Narwhal") was thoroughly tested before the big day. Dress rehearsals were conducted weeks in advance, and the team developed procedures for every possible mode of failure that they could think of. On the day, those investments paid off, and the system functioned as planned.

At Romney headquarters, the story was different. Users of the system (called "Orca") reported outages, slow responses, and other technical issues that prevented them from using it effectively. At times, connectivity to the field workers was lost; according to reports, at one point the internet service provider (ISP) connecting the system to the Internet shut down access because the ISP thought that the high level of traffic was caused by a "denial of service" type attack. The frustration of the users rose rapidly, and trying to fix the problems took critical resources away from managing the campaign.

The day after the election, stories about the system began to surface. At the core of the problem was a failure to subject the system (or its users and support personnel) to the same level of testing as Narwhal had received. There had been no full dress rehearsals, and Election Day was the first time Orca had been run on the full set of systems infrastructure used at Romney's Boston headquarters. In addition, reports indicated that the campaign workers had failed to communicate with their ISP; as a result, the ISP was not expecting the high volume of traffic that would be flowing.

Would Orca have changed the outcome of the election had it worked more smoothly? Probably not. Obama's margin of victory was significant, and aggregated polling sites (such as Votamatic and Nate Silver's *New York Times* FiveThirtyEight blog) had been predicting the precise margin of victory for some time. The Orca story is, however, a reminder to all organizations of the need to ensure that they thoroughly test critical operational systems before releasing them into their live environments. Failure to do so can dramatically raise stress levels at critical times, can divert resources away from core business functions, and can lead to embarrassing public relations failures.

Contributing factors as reported in the press:
- Failure to perform dress rehearsals.
- Failure to plan for peak performance system requests.
- Failure to stress test a new system in its full operational environment.
- Failure to inform key stakeholders.
- Lack of risk management.

Source: © Calleam Consulting Ltd. 2012 with permission.

Ask these key questions when using Rule 5

- Has the project been broken into smaller subprojects, to allow early deliverables or early wins that can be publicized?
- Have innovative or other new activities been tested to learn what works and what does not?
- Have key performance indicators been established to track implementation, and have data been fed back to the project team?
- Does the team meet regularly to discuss implementation data and, where needed, to adjust project design or execution planning?
- Are mistakes part of a learning program, or is blame assigned immediately?

Laufer, Alexander. 2009. *Breaking the Code of Project Management*. New York: Palgrave Macmillan.

Schaffer, Robert H., and Ronald Ashkenas. 2005. *Rapid Results! How 100-Day Projects Build the Capacity for Large-Scale Change*. San Francisco: Jossey Bass.

State of Gujarat, India. 2011. Government website, March 31.

Tugend, Alina. 2011. *Better by Mistake: The Unexpected Benefits of Being Wrong*. New York: Riverhead Books.

Use the five rules to avoid project failure

Have you ever worked on a project that left you exhausted at the end of each day? Despite the fact that you and your team are working long hours, you never seem to move forward. Moreover, no one at the top of the organization seems particularly to care about your project. Your team leader cannot get the attention of the senior manager, and that manager is always canceling review meetings. Even worse, you find out that someone else has already solved a seemingly intractable problem you have been dealing with. If you only had the benefit of this information, it would have saved the time and energy of your team.

Working hard is not the same as *getting to project success* (Kusek and Rist 2004). We know now that even with a good technical design and a dedicated, hardworking project team, a lot can go wrong. A World Bank colleague, Shabih Ali Mohib, recently confided that in all his years of painstakingly designing development projects to succeed, he finally realized that when they do not, it is because of poor implementation. In fact, we have not found one failed project that did not break at least one of the rules we have set forth in this guide. We have also found, by interacting closely with the project team, that an opportunity always exists to put the effort back on track if we first understand which of the five rules may have been broken.

A province in South Africa used the *Five Rules to Avoid Failure* to try to get a project back on track. The project director of a new initiative to introduce outcome-based management in one of the South African states asked the University of Witwatersrand (WITS), in Johannesburg, to help analyze why the project was not moving as fast as everyone had hoped. Stephen Porter, acting director of the WITS South Africa CLEAR (Center on Learning for Evaluation and Results) project, met with the project director and his team to understand what was keeping them from successfully implementing the initiative, which was led by an individual with years of experience heading complicated government projects. The director voiced a number of concerns, such as the lack of sufficient resources and a seeming inability of team members to work well together or to trust one another.

Porter decided to use the Five Rules to understand what forces might be causing the problems. The qualitative methodology selected for the analysis was focus groups. The groups consisted of project managers, team leaders, and province staff members who were involved in the project or who were stakeholders from inside the province with an interest in the effort. A number of group meetings were held to discuss how the project was adhering (or not) to the Five Rules:

1. Make it about the *how*
2. Keep your champions close but your critics closer
3. Informal networks matter—use them
4. Unclog the pipes
5. Build the ship as it sails

The assignment given to each group was to be open and free with their comments and, when they cited a problem, to identify a possible fix as well. This requirement kept the complaining to a minimum, while empowering the group to be part of the solution. A facilitator recorded the groups' findings and recommendations and then noted how many times a particular problem was identified and how many times a particular solution was proposed. These items were then graphed to show which problem was cited most often, as well as how often each of the solutions was cited.

Findings were surprising to management but not to staff

Three findings were consistent: (a) a high level of distrust across the organization, (b) serious bottlenecks in moving work through the approval process, and (c) a lack of constituency groups to support the effort.

The group participants noted a high level of distrust in the organization. Many people were from distinctly different cultures with a history of poor interpersonal relations. Distinct expert and trust networks existed that were not considered when the project was designed. Moreover, the formal organization chart did not encourage information to flow freely across the organization. As a result, staff members were not always able to receive information they needed to do their jobs. Thus, they typically relied on informal networks to move work through the organization.

The focus groups voiced a need to identify and remove bottlenecks in the report approval process. Here, work was regularly pushed back for multiple reworkings and often sat in in-boxes before any action was taken. This situation was partially related to the lack of willingness to delegate but was also caused by the lack of a sense of urgency to get the work done.

Finally, the groups were concerned that the state's commitment to introducing outcome-based management was not supported by champions who could help lead and sustain the effort.

WITS briefed the project team about the findings of the study and the recommendations that the focus groups had offered. The director was surprised at the consistency of the findings. He also listened closely to the suggested remedies, particularly the ones on how to reestablish trust in the organization. Follow-up discussions and actions were planned.

The fail-safe manager has a checklist for avoiding project failure

Problems are inevitable in any development project; failure is not. Our goal has been to show, from a management orientation, how project failures germinate and take root and where to look for the sources of potential failure in any project. With the foregoing in mind, the following assessment checklist can be applied to any project to guard against project failures. Obviously, a simple checklist is no substitute for alert and insightful management or strong systems to track whether a project is being implemented to achieve its intended results. It does not eliminate the need to be willing to make midcourse adjustments when the need arises, but it can help managers spot the potential for failure in a project, which is the first step to avoiding it.

The *Five Rules to Avoid Failure Checklist*, or "the Rules," is intended to be used as a self-assessment tool. Will a project fail if just one rule is not followed? Will it take two or the entire five? We think that neglecting to follow any one of the rules will provide an opening for failure to take root. Thus, understanding where your project is against any one or all of the rules provides an opportunity to put things back on track. We believe that fail-safe or mindful managers want to be alert to the possibility of failure. Using the checklist is one way to begin.

Five Rules to Avoid Project Failure Checklist

Rule 1. Make it about the *how*.

1. What development problem is the project trying to intervene in?
2. What would success look like for a key target group of stakeholders?
3. Do the project activities follow sound project logic?
4. Has a project implementation plan been developed that is aligned to development objectives?
5. Has an activity breakdown plan been developed?
6. Have resources been estimated, and are they available for each task?
7. How will each task be managed? Has an owner been assigned?

Rule 2. Keep your champions close but your critics closer.

1. Who is the project's most important champion?
2. What is motivating him or her?
3. Have other key stakeholders been identified?
4. Has a power mapping been done, and have the most important (interested and powerful) stakeholders been identified?
5. What is the plan for managing relations with the most important champions?
6. What is the plan for managing relations with powerful critics?
7. Who in the team is developing key messages and making certain they are understood by stakeholders?
8. What is the plan for alerting project decision makers if serious problems occur with a particular stakeholder?

Rule 3. Informal networks matter—use them.

1. Have you identified the informal networks within your organization?
2. Do you have a sense of how they operate and who is involved?
3. Are they useful or detrimental to accomplishing your organization's goals?
4. What can be done to strengthen them?

5. How can you use them to your strategic advantage—as sources of information, as informal communications networks, or as vehicles for streamlining and speeding up work?
6. Would they help or hurt if the organization faced a crisis?

Rule 4. Unclog the pipes.

1. Do you understand the processes involved in each of your project's key activities?
2. Which work processes in the project account for the greatest cost?
3. Have you mapped them, even in a simple way?
4. Do you know which steps take the longest, and why?
5. Have you considered making someone in the project responsible for process management—for making sure that bottlenecks are identified and eliminated and that the process is monitored for the development of new bottlenecks?
6. What possible bottlenecks are simply not fixable, and are other solutions possible for the problem?

Rule 5. Build the ship as it sails.

1. Has the project been broken into smaller subprojects to allow early deliverables or early wins that can be publicized?
2. Have innovative or other new activities been tested to learn what works and what does not?
3. Have performance indicators been established to track implementation, and have the data been fed back to the project team?
4. Does the team meet regularly to discuss implementation data and the status of the project?
5. Where needed, is the project design or execution plan adjusted?
6. Are mistakes part of a learning process, or is blame assigned immediately?

Reference

Kusek, Jody Zall, and Ray C. Rist. 2004. *Ten Steps to a Results-Based Monitoring and Evaluation System*. Washington, DC: World Bank.

Afterword

We live in a world of increasing complexity and extraordinary international development challenges. The demands on international organizations to develop sound projects that deliver the results promised have never been greater. At the same time, the potential for failure has also never been greater. In this environment, things going wrong are an all-too-common modern management experience. Development projects inherently involve trade-offs between project goals, and other pressures can underlie budget considerations.

Pressed for time, the client or donor manager often makes a hasty decision that remedies one problem but creates myriad new problems. The list of potential problems is seemingly endless. Although projects are launched with the best intentions, too often managers court failure in predictable patterns—through simple confusion and misperception, short attention spans, failure to collect and understand performance data, and unwillingness to change tactics.

Not all is lost, however. Despite the potential for failure that is part of any large development project, managers can learn to recognize defective organizational and management behaviors and to correct them. Our goal in this guide is to encourage managers to recognize that an understanding of the sources of and potential for project failure is, in fact, part of a strategy for promoting success. By understanding how failure arises within a policy or project, we can understand how the possibility of failure can be reduced or eliminated.

Begin with our simple assessment of the major sources of project failure, but do not stop there. We know that these sources may not be the same weakness categories that you may have identified as the ones that cause failure. However, we believe we have found, in our collective 80 years of managing projects, those weaknesses that are both important and most often overlooked.

Our goal is to instill in managers the certain knowledge that failure is a potential in any public project and to encourage mindful, or what we call fail-safe management. Problems will always be part of any project, but they can be identified and controlled before they escalate to the point where they produce a full-scale breakdown. The best managers recognize the stress points in their projects. They collect and analyze data with an eye toward developing problems. They admit problems as those concerns arise, and they are flexible in their response. When mindfulness replaces mindlessness in our project management, then success will replace failure. It is that simple—and that difficult.

—Jody, Marelize, and Billy

www.ingramcontent.com/pod-product-compliance
Lightning Source LLC
Chambersburg PA
CBHW082109210326
41599CB00033B/6648